AF539973

ECONOMIC DEVELOPMENT
AND
PROBLEM OF DISPLACEMENT

Edited by

S.N. Tripathy

ANMOL PUBLICATIONS PVT. LTD.
NEW DELHI - 110 002 (INDIA)

ANMOL PUBLICATIONS PVT. LTD.
4374/4B, Ansari Road, Daryaganj
New Delhi - 110 002
Ph.: 3261597, 3278000
Visit us at: www.anmolbooks.com

Economic Development and Problem of Displacement
© Reserved

First Edition, 2003

ISBN 81-261-1384-7

[The responsibility for the facts stated, conclusions reached and plagiarism, if any, in the articles contained herein is entirely that of the respective Author(s). And the Publisher bears no responsibility for them, whatsoever.]

PRINTED IN INDIA

Published by J.L. Kumar for Anmol Publications Pvt. Ltd., New Delhi - 110 002 and Printed at Tarun Offset Press, Delhi.

Contents

Preface vii

1. Development, Displacement and Outcome of Large Dam Projects in Orissa: A Case of Upper Kolab Dam 1
   —*Dr. Bipin Kumar Jojo*

2. Impact of Development Induced Displacement on Tribals 35
   —*Dr. S.N. Tripathy*

3. Behavioural Concerns of the Displaced during Development 42
   —*Dr. A. Ramakrishna*

4. Sounds of Silence: A Sterile Promontory of Development and Displacement in the Narmada Valley 52
   —*Dr. Prashant Negi*

5. Large Dams, Sustainable Development and Displacement 85
   —*Dr. B. Eswar Rao Patnaik*

6. Land Acquisition for Development Projects and Rehabilitation of Displaced Persons (A Case Study of NALCO, Orissa) 99
   —*Dr. C.R. Das*

7. Displacement and Development: The Land Acquisition Act 1894 (As Amended in 1984) 115
   —*Dr. G.B. Nath*

8. Displacement and Deprivation of Tribal People in Orissa — 128
—Dr. Nilakantha Panigrahi

9. Rehabilitation and Development for Hirakud Oustees — 151
—Dr. Chitrasen Pasayat

10. The Political Economy of Development and Displacement — 166
—Dr. Deepak K. Mishra

11. Displacement and Development: A Cost Benefit Analysis — 174
—Dr. S.N. Behera & Smt. Ranjita Kumari Mohanty

12. Problems of Displacement and Development — 187
—Dr. S.N. Tripathy

Index — 194

Preface

In view of agricultural economy like India, the execution of river valley projects assume paramount significance. Having the dubious distinction of the largest number of river valley projects in the world, our country through Planned Development Policy has incurred crores of rupees in the development projects. The river valley projects have created several advantages like providing additional irrigation facilities, increased crop production, power generation, increased availability of water for domestic and industrial purposes, controlling floods, generating employment avenues, development of infrastructure etc. Though boosting the level of income of the local inhabitants through the implementation of river valley dam projects have been advocated but the consequent of results of displacement, injudicious use of finance, misappropriation, unruption, submergence of vast tracts of rable and forest, wide spread of water logging, soil-erosion, siltation are the disadvantages originated due to river dam projetcs.

It is a matter of deep concern that the fruits of development could not be precolated to the tribal and poverty stricken people, despite our planned efforts. In the name of development in all irrigation projects, hydroelectricity projects, industrial and mining belts, the local inhabitants have been victimised. The interest of the uprooted tribals and weakers sections have been relegated to background because of defective rehabilitation and compensation policy. The problem of tribals is mainly linked with the backwardness of the tribal area, poverty of the people and the nature of development policy. The innumerable victims of the development projects are adivasis, dalits and tribals. Hence, the resettlement of oustees must be made forthwith and all displacement issues must take into note the socio-economic and environmental impacts. Moreover, displacement is a violation of people's most fundamental right and we too recognise the valuable price paid and sacrifice made by three crores of uprooted inhabitants of developments projetcs area.

Instead of large dam projects, water-shed management, tanks and other locally supportive and environmentally conducive measures be adopted as innovative techniques to safeguard the interest of oiiginal inhabitants and tribals.

The present work covers wide spectrum of issues pertaining to developmental projetcs undertaken in India since Independence by eminent authors and social scientists. This work could not have been made possible without the contribution of papers by the researchers and hence, the editor expresses his deep sense of gratitude to all of them.

It is hoped that these papers focussing new light to the existing developmental policy will endeavour to find out new policy paradigms to mitigate the problems and will show a direction for future courses of action.

— S.N. Tripathy

1

Development, Displacement and Outcome of Large Dam Projects in Orissa: A Case Study of Upper Kolab Dam

— *Dr. Bipin Kumar Jojo* *

Introduction

After Independence, India planned and aimed for fast economic growth along with other third world countries. Modernization and development emerged as dominant ideologies in the planned economy. The central planning and public sector undertakings were set up to give a new thrust for the creation of modern economic infrastructure for heavy industries, hydro-electric dams and production of chemical fertilizers and insecticides etc. All these capital intensive establishment were considered as modern temples of India and symbols of development to follow by the architect of modern India Jawaharlal Nehru. On the day of lying foundation stone of the Hirakud Dam, the first large dam in the post -independent India, he said, "I am vastly interested in all these river valley – the Mahanadi, Damodar valley, Kosi, Bhakra, and others, for I feel that they will be foundation of all future development in India. They will prevent disastrous flood and soil erosion, they will bring large areas under cultivation and will thus increase the food supply of India and they will also produce hydro-electric power and thus help

---

* *Dr. Jojo, Faculty, Department of Social Welfare Administration, Tata Institute of Social Sciences, Deonar, Mumbai–400088.*

in the rapid development of industry" (CBIP, 1989: 1). From the first five year plan onwards, there have been plan outlays for the construction of major dams and creation of irrigation potential investment on the river projects. At the same time, international funding agencies are also funding many projects in India. There are 3634 large dams in different states of India out of which, 696 are under construction (CWC, 1990: 69).

This chapter is divided into three sections. The first section looks at the irrigation and power projects and extent of the utilisation these resources. Second section reviews briefly about the displacement and resettlement and rehabilitation situation in Orissa. The final section deals with the evolution and comeout of Upper Kolab Multipurpose Project.

I

RIVER DAM PROJECTS IN ORISSA

The Orissa State is one of the poor states in the country in spite of having vast amount of natural resources like forest, water, mineral and fertile land. After Independence, planned development initiated the process of exploitation of natural resources. Hence, industries, mines, dams have been constructed in different parts of the state.

The construction of dam has become an integral part of industrialisation and other development processes in the state as well as in the country. Major rivers of the state are Mahanadi, Brahmani, Salandi, Budhabalnga, Subernarekha, Rusikrulya etc., which flow into the Bay of Bengal. In Orissa, since 1901, there has been many as 149 medium and large dams, out of which 18 are under construction, ranging in height from 10 to 71 meter and length from 45 to 6215.85 meter (CWC, 1990: 87-90). The purpose of all these dams include irrigation except one dam, which has been purely built for hydro-electricity generation purpose. Few projects are multipurpose catering to irrigation, hydro-electricity generation and water supply. Though irrigation and hydro-electricity are the main attraction of these projects, the state is yet to provide these facilities to all the people in the state.

Irrigation

Irrigation plays a major role in boosting agriculture production. The 8th Plan (1992-97) outlay under major and medium irrigation sector has been finalized at Rs. 2614.33 crores with a target to create additional irrigation potential of 249.55 thousand hectares. Kharif under state sector and 33.92 thousand hect. Kharif as central sector (Mahapatra, 1994: 8).

Table 1

Net Irrigation Area as Percentage of Net sown Area (in Percentage)

Year	1971-72	1981-82	1990-91
Orissa	14.8	19.5	30.7
All India	22.6	31.6	33.3

Source: CMIE, Basic Statistics relating to State of India, Sep. 1994, Table 3.8

Table above shows that there has been a steady increase in the amount of irrigation over the years in Orissa. But still, it is below the all India average. In the last ten years (1981-82 to 1990-91) the increase in the amount of irrigation in Orissa has been significant.

The above table shows that canals, tanks and wells are the only sources of the irrigation in Orissa. Though the percentage of total irrigated area in Orissa is very small (maximum 4.1%), canals and tanks irrigate more compared to, in all of India. The wells irrigate 38.3% of the area while the all India figure is 51%. A massive investment in the 7th has been made and 8th five year plan has been made for increasing the irrigation potential of the state.

Table 1 shows that only 46.29% of irrigation potential has been harnessed upto 1991-92 from the total irrigation potential in Orissa where as the same has been 73.20% for all or India. Out of the irrigation potential created, 89.68% in Orissa and 91.10% in all or India has been utilised. The creation of irrigation potential through all the projects as well as their utilisation, are less than the ultimate irrigation potential and the potential created respectively.

Table 2
Source of Irrigation (% distribution)

Sources	Canals			Tanks			Wells Sources			Other of all India			Total as %		
Year	71-72	81-82	90-91	71-72	81-82	90-91	71-72	81-82	90-91	71-72	81-82	90-91	71-72	81-82	90-92
Orissa	64.4	65.9	46.7	20.3	17.0	14.9	15.3	17.1	38.3	00.0	00.0	00.0	2.7	3.0	4.1
All India	41.6	39.2	35.7	11.8	8.2	6.8	38.9	46.5	51.0	7.7	6.1	6.5	100	100	100

Source: CMIE, Sep. 1995, Table 3. 10-2

Table 3
Development of Irrigation Potential and Utilization upto 1991-92 (% distribution)

Irrigation Potential Created as % of ultimate irrigation potential			Utilization as % of irrigation potential created	
Source	Orissa	India	Orissa	India
Major and medium projects	40.90%	56.11%	90.51%	89.07%
Minor projects	54.29%	91.36%	88.70%	92.43%
Total	46.29%	73.20%	89.68%	91.10%

Source: CMIE, Basic Statistics relating to the Indian Economy.

Power

At the end of 1975-76, the installed capacity of power in Orissa was 863 M.W. representing 4.29% of the installed capacity of the country and in 1993-94 the installed capacity became 1932 M.W. which is 2.26% of the installed capacity of the country, marking a significant decrease (Dir. of Economics and Statistics, 1995, Table 9.1). The installed capacity has increased with the establishment of different hydro-power projects. But the firm power has not been able to achieve its fullest capacity. The following tables shows the installed capacity and firm power, of power projects in Orissa.

Table 4

Installed Capacity and Firm Power Projects in Orissa during the Year 1993-94 (in M. W.)

Power projects	Installed capacity	Firm power	Firm power to Installed Capacity (%)
A. State Sector			
(a) Hydro-power project			
1. Hirakud	307.5	134	43.58
2. Balimela	360.0	135	37.50
3. Machhkund (Orissa share)	34.5	34	98.55
4. Rengali	250.0	86	34.40
5. Uppar Kolab	320.0	95	29.69
Total Hydro Projects	1272.0	484	38.05
(b) Thermal Power Projects			
TTPS (stage I & II)	460.0	184	40.00
Total State Sector	1732.0	668	38.27
B. Central Sector			
1. Farakka STPP (stage I in West Bengal)	75.0	42	56.00
2. Chukka HE project in Bhutan	36.5	19	52.05
Total Central Sector	111.5	61	54.73
Total Availbility of power within the state by the end of 1993-94	1843.5	729	39.54

From the table 4 it is evident that against 1843.5 M.W. of installed capacity the firm power was only 729 (39.54%) M.W.

in the year 1993-94. It is further evident that none of the State sector projects was able to achieve 50% or more firm power with reference to their installed capacity except Machhkund where the achievement was as high as 98.55%. On the whole, considering both thermal and hydropower projects, the State could achieve firm power only to the tune of 38.27% of the installed capacity in the State sector projects by 1993-94. Considering the Central sector projects i.e. Farakka STPP Stage-I in West Bengal and Chukka H.E. project in Bhutan, the target for receiving power by Orissa was to the extent of 111.5 M.W. against which the state has received power to the extent of 61 M.W., which accounted for 54.73% of the installed capacity.

The projects either in irrigation or power generation are showing the result below their capacity. In spite of that, more and more investment is being made on these projects though many ongoing projects are facing the bottleneck of financial constraint.

Table 5

Percentage Consumption of Power in Different Sectors

Year	Total Consumption in M.W.	Domestic	Commercial	Industrial	Public Lighting
1.	2.	3.	4.	5.	6.
1985-86	378	10.71	2.83	73.08	0.40
1993-94	691	25.34	5.67	54.03	0.56
Year	Irrigation & agriculture	Railways	Public Water Works	Bulk Supply	Total
1.	7.	8.	9.	10.	11.
1985-86	2.27	4.75	1.90	4.06	100
1993-94	5.64	2.71	1.87	4.18	100

Source: Directorate of Economics and Statistics, 1995, Table 9.7.

The above table represents the pattern of power consumption in Orissa in terms of percentage. Consumption of energy in domestic sector has been steeped up from 10.71% in 1985-86 to 25.34% in 1993-94. Similarly, commercial consumption has risen from 2.83% in 1985-86 to 5.67% in 1993-

94. Industrial sector has taken a lion's share of the total power consumed in the economy ranging from 73.08% (the highest) in 1985-86 to 54.30% in 1993-94. Percentage of power consumed in public lighting system has reminded more or less around 0.5% since 1985-86 to 1994-95. Irrigation and Agriculture had absorbed power to the extent of 2.27% in 1985-86 to 5.64 % in 1993-94. Power consumed by the Railways has declined steadily over the decade i.e. from 1985-86 to 1994-95. It was 4.75% in 1985-86, and 2.71% in 1993-94. Public Water Works consumed power ranging from 1.90% in 1985-86 to 1.87% in 1993-94. The percentage of power consumed in bulk supply (miscellaneous) category has remained more or less around 4% in these two years. From the above table it is further evident that the percentage of power consumed in industrial sector was the highest in the state and this is more conspicuous from the years 1985-86 to 1994-95. Since rural electrification programme has gained momentum after 1985-86, percentage of power consumed in this sector grew steadily over the years. Irrigation and agriculture which ought to have consumed sizeable quantities of power have not done so, since its percentage has never exceed 6.0% in any of the years i.e. from 1985-86 to 1994-95.

II

DISPLACEMENT AND RESETTLEMENT AND REHABILITATION PROCESS IN ORISSA

Displacement and Resettlement and rehabilitation is not a new phenomenon in Orissa. It stated way back in the 1940s and 1950s with the construction of Machkund hydroproject on the Duduma river in Koratput district. The Maharaja of Jeypore got the idea of this project in the 1920s. However, on 14.1.1946, an agreement was reached between the Ex-Madras State and Orissa regarding development of hydropower on Duduma. The project was undertaken with the condition that its cost and benefits were to be shared by Andhra Pradesh and Orissa. It was the first major dam project in Orissa. Dalua (1993) mentions that there are no data documented to show the magnitude of the displacement due to construction of this project. It again mentions that there was no clearly laid down rehabilitation policy, and hence the project authorities remained content with payment of compensation only for the property lost by the people evicted.

But Mahapatra (1989:96) says that 2938 families were displaced by the project, out of which 1500 (51%) of them were tribals, 300 (10.21%) of them were scheduled castes and rest of them were other castes. Only 600 families were rehabilitated (450 tribals and 150 others). Similarly Stanely (1996: 1533-1534) finds that the displaced people were rehabilitated in an environment similar to that from which they were displaced and so adapted themselves to their new surroundings. The displaced people were offered "land for land" provision of rehabilitation.

The response of the people towards the construction of the Machkund project and the compensation and rehabilitation is hardly known to any body. However Stanely (1996) says that in two villages, the people had decided against leaving their birthplace and represented a memorandum to the Chief Minister and the local government officials. The people had decided to lead an agitation against the project. Ultimately, the villagers got settled for higher compensation and better rehabilitation than originally envisaged. No further information is available about the nature and extent of people's response towards the project.

Hirakud Dam Project

Hirakud dam is the first multipurpose project of independent India and is situated in the Sambalpur district of Orissa. It displaced 22144 families in 249 villages in Orissa, besides affecting 36 villages in Madhya Pradesh (Dalua, 1993:40). In the absence of any policy guidelines on the rehabilitation, the affected people were paid compensation for the land and property. The government reclaimed some land for the affected people to be resettled. It was found from the figures or evaluation in 1954-55 that about 11 per cent of the land owner from the submerged area settled on the government reclaimed land and the rest made their own arrangement because the reclaimed area was on a hilly slope and near the forest areas which was not suitable for cultivation (Patanaik, Das, Mishra, 1987:55). The displaced people are still waiting for the promised provision by the government. Many of them have been experiencing multiple displacement due to the coal mines in the region.

There was strong opposition against the project by the local people. The political leaders, ex-bureaucrats and the landlord took an active role in the protest against the project. The state Congress leadership managed to divide the leaders of the protest and many withdrew from the agitation. As a result, the project plan went ahead for the implementation. The people's protest did not have any impact on the government which went on to construct the project. Neither did it do any thing to improve the rehabilitation provisions for the displaced people.

Salandi Irrigation Project

The Salandi Irrigation Project was the first major irrigation project in the state funded by World Bank. This project commenced in Keonjhar district. Despite the funding of World Bank, the resettlement and rehabilitation guidelines of the Bank was not implemented in this project (Dalua, 1993). The affected people were treated in the similar ways as in the case of the Hirakud dam. There is no information available regarding the response of the people towards the project.

Balimela Dam Project

The Balimela Dam Project was the second largest hydro-electricity project in Koraput district. This commenced in 1962–63 and was completed in 1977 displacing 2000 families (Dalua, 1991). The Resettlement and Rehabilitation guidelines of the Hirakud dam was repeated again in this project. Here too, there is no information available regarding the people's response towards the project.

The Rengali Dam Project

The construction of the Rengali Dam Project in the early seventies, paved the way for the historical chapter of

Resettlement and Rehabilitation in Orissa. This project displaced more than ten thousand families. The people had witnessed the miseries of the affected people of Hirakud Dam in the same region. A strong resistance was started against the construction of the Rengali Dam. The Government of Orissa was compelled by the agitation of the families to be displaced by the Rengali Dam Reservoir area, to formulate a rehabilitation policy for the oustees in December 1973 (Mahapatra, 1989: 87) with the resolution No. 35054 dated 6.12.1973. This was further elaborated and developed into a uniform policy to be adopted for all major and medium irrigation projects by the resolution No. 13169 dated 20.4.1977. The people's resistance against the project forced the government to liberalise the Resettlement and Rehabilitation provision further. The same policy was adopted in case of the Upper Kolab Project.

Uppar Indravati Hydro Project

The construction of the Upper Indravati Hydro Project aided by the World Bank, initiated another chapter in the history of R & R in Orissa. This is an ongoing project which has been started in 1978-79. The four dams across the river Indravati and its tributaries Patogoda, Kapur and Muvan would form a single reservoir submerging 44 villages in Koraput district and 51 villages in Kalahandi district. The figures of the number of families displaced vary as per source available. One of the sources mentioned that 5725 families are to be displaced out of which 1630 families are tribal and 538 families are scheduled castes (Mahapatra, 1989:86).

The dismissal picture of R & R in Orissa as well as in the whole country, attracted the attention of the advocacy groups, social activists, environmentalists and many scientists. The Narmada Bachao Andolan, brought out the apathetic attitude of the state and central government regarding the compensation and R & R of affected people to the attention of national and international human rights organisations, and other environment organisations. Also the World Bank came under severe corners, the World Bank developed its guidelines and insisted on governments receiving the bank's aid toward policy formulation on the R & R of project affected persons. Since the Uppar Indiravati Project is aided by the World Bank, the government of Orissa had to adhere the bank guidelines on R & R. Many advocacy groups and NGOs in the State also raised R & R and environmental concerns while taking up river projects and industries. As a result, the government of Orissa was forced to enact the Orissa Resettlement and Rehabilitation of Project Affected Policy, 1944. However, this policy is not applicable to the past projects.

III
UPPER KOLAB MULTI-PURPOSE PROJECT

General Characteristics of the Area

The Uppar Kolab Multi-purpose Project is constructed across the river Kolab. The dam is situated at the village Koronga (between the latitude of 18 degree – 47 degree N and longitude of 82 degree – 37 degree E) of Koraput block and district in Orissa. It is 22 kms. away from Koraput as well as Jeypore towns and 543 kms. from the state capital.

The river Kolab is tributary of river Godavari. It originates in Eastern Ghats in Koraput district from RL 1200 m. on its course, it is joined by a number of tributaries like Guradi and Karandi. In the lower reaches it is known as 'Sabari'. It has got legendary importance for the people of Koraput district. The river flows through a series of rapid and small falls in the course, due to the hilly regions. The biggest fall is located at village Baghra about 5 kms. down stream of the dam site which used to be a picnic spot for the people of the region. The river forms the common boundary of Orissa and Madhya Pradesh from village Godoghati for some distance and then flows in turn in both the states and again forms the boundary. At the down reach, the river Sabari joins river Sileruat the place called Motu which is the common point of three states– Orissa, Madhya Pradesh and Andhra Pradesh. The combined river after confluence with Sileru is also called 'Sabari' and it joins the Godavari, a few kilometers downstream of

Bhadrachalam. During floods, the flow is generally contained within the banks and therefore there is practically no flood threat in this river.

Topography

The topography of the district is diverse. It is full of hilly ranges, dense forests and patches of plain landscapes in between valleys. The Nowrangpur sub-division is the only main flat area, except for the forests in the west of Jeypore tahsil where there are low hills. Due to its fertile lands and this population this region has become the principal grainary of the district. The district is full of natural resources like land, water, forests. Due to its hilly topography and river basins, it has got high potential of hydro-electricity production.

Socio-economic Characteristics

It is tribal populated district with 55.22% of tribals as per the 1999 census. Among the tribals—Parajs, Gadabas, Kondhs, Bhottadas, Koyas are the major ones. The Bondas and the Didayi are the primitive tribes of the state who are still isolated from the main society.

The shifting cultivation is widely practised in this district. It has been attributed as one of the main reason for deforestation in the district. The state government is taking consistent efforts for afforestation and stop shifting cultivation. The Koraput district accounts for 49.36% of total area under shifting cultivation in different tribal areas of Orissa (Patnaik 1988, Table 3).

The tribals of the district are found at varying stages of development. One of the reports of the Commissioners of SCs and STs found as many as 13 tribes of the district to be the weakest and primitive on the ground of low percentage of literacy, unmodified occupation, remoteness or inaccessibility of the habitat and dependence on shifting cultivation (Mahapatro, 1988: 24). Due to the high concentration of tribals and under-development of the district, it is considered essential for under tribal sub-plans to focus on development programmes. There are integrated tribal development agencies to undertake special programmes in the district. Besides this two micro project Bonda Development Agency and Dongria Kondh Development Agency are functioning for concentrated socio-economic development of Bonda and Dongria Kondh tribes in the district. The Koraput district is one of the four districts of Orissa currently under the Prime Minister's Special Assistance Programme.

Industrialization

The district has high potential for industrial development. The construction of National Highway, the broad gauge railway lines and other infrastructural development has accelerated the industrial development in the 1980s. The construction of Machhkund and Balimela hydro-electric projects are the initial milestones in the industrial development in the district. The Aero-engine factory at Sunabeda, NALCO at Damonjodi, J.K. paper mill near Jeypore, Fero Manganese factory near Raigada and excavation of different mines and many forest based industries are now situated in the district. In the year 1987-88, there were 6626 persons employed in the factory sector (Directorate of Economics and Statistics, 1990-91:4). Due to the lack of availability of required manpower, local migration is taking place in order to fill up the industrial job opportunities. As a result, the local people are displaced by the establishment of industries on one hand and being deprived and dispossessed of their own resources on the other.

Koraput district contributes a major share in the electricity production in the state. The industrial sector consumed 58.42% of the share whereas agriculture and irrigation consumed only 2.41% in the year 1989-90. However, the number of villages electrified was 40%. Similarly, irrigation potential created in Kharif season to net area sown was only 16.5% in the same year (Directorate of Economics and Statistics 1990-91, Tables 10.01 & 1.01).

Plan of the Upper Kolab Project

The project plan envisaged that primarily it would produce hydro-electric and create irrigation potential for the Jeypore

Plateau. Besides, this, it would provide the water for the use of Jeypore Municipality. The reservoir would help for the development of fishery and the dam site could be developed as a tourist place of the region. The downstream never experienced any severe floods, so controlling flood was not needed. Moreover, due to the topography of the river flow, navigation was not possible through the reservoir.

The construction material like stone, sand, earth, chips could be available in the local areas. The nearest railways station Rayagada was 135 kms. away and National Highway 43 was 10 kms. away from the dam site. With the construction of approach road to dam site from the national highway, the communication problems were to be solved. The other construction materials like cement, steel and plants, machineries could be transported easily to the dam site. The Department of Irrigation and Power of Government of Orissa being the controlling authority of the project would provide the skilled and experienced personnel require the technical assistance from the Central Water and Power Commission at different stages of work.

Most of the major works in the project were to be undertaken by the different construction firms and departmental agencies. The machines and plants were to be bought from the indigenous market. Many of the machines from the completing Balimela project were to be used in this project.

Keeping this in view, a construction schedule was prepared providing minimum time for the planning and designing work, two years for delivery of power house machineries, four years for generating equipment and three and half year for erection (Irrigation & Power Department, 1988: 41).

The project was supposed to displace the population of 40 villages with 2113 houses [Irrigation and Power Department, 1972, Statement A-15(a)]. The displaced were to be resettled in the command areas of the project with all modern facilities and amenities.

The objective of the Upper Kolab Project was fast economic growth and removal of regional imbalances in different development plans. The tribal areas of different states which happened to be rich in natural resources namely, forest, minerals and water got attention by the government. Many large and medium scale industries came up to exploit the existing natural resources. It is important to understand the political-economy of the different hydro-electricity projects in general and specifically, the Upper Kolab Multi-purpose Project in particular.

The power production in the state was not able to meet the demand even after the construction of the Machhkund, Hirakud Stage I and II hydro project and Talcher Thermal station. These projects served only a few areas. The industries grew up where the power was available i.e. industrial area of Hirakud, Rourkela, Joda, Chowdwar and Jajpur road. Due to the abundance of mineral resources in the state most of the industries are electro-metallurgical. The creation of new industries at Talcher, Jajpur Road, Jeypore, Paradip Port and the increasing demand for the power which was more than the production of the newly complete Balimela project, Machkund project, and increased amount of power production from the Hirakud and Tachler Thermal Project. The growing demand of power for the state required to generate more power.

Besides, there are other reasons also strongly supporting the demand for more power production. The Central Water and Power Commission conducted seven annual power surveys from 1969-70 to 1974-75 to study the load fore-caste in the state. The study came out with the findings that there was annual demand growth rate of 15 per cent. The other studies by the Expert Committee on Power of the Joint Planning Board of the Planning Commission and the Ministry of Irrigation and Power and also the Government of India in its Decade Plan for Power (1971-81) recommended towards achieving the annual growth rate of 15% for Orissa Power System (Irrigation and Power Department, 1972: 45-49). It was envisaged that apart from the supply to the demand of Orissa loads, it should also be able to achieve inter-state transfer of power. This formed apart of system load for the purpose of planning. Even though the firm power and energy and capability of the hydro-station is lower compared to thermal station, they reach peak capacity sometimes, especially during floods. Then the hydro stations provide irrigation to the agriculture and checks the floods. The exploitation of the available water resources could be good combination with the thermal stations supplementing each other in the firm power. They hydro-stations of Orissa would offer valuable backing to the eastern region where most of the power generation was thermal. The coordination between the thermal and hydro-power production would help for the flexibility in production and manage the power requirements of the region. Then, the study of the energy required and available between 1975 and 1979 showed that the energy available was always below the requirement (ibid). It was predicated that Orissa would face serious energy crisis towards the end of 1976-77, unless the generation was increased with new schemes. Therefore, it was proposed to take up the hydro projects of Kolab/Indravati and expansion of Talcher Thermal Station for the growing needs of the state.

The power potential of different rivers in Koraput and adjacent district were planned. They would create irrigation potential and make the project multi-purpose, and thus reduce the cost of the power. The low cost of power would help the establishment and expansion of electrometallurgical industries in the state and also provide irrigation in the Koratpur district. Keeping all these in view, the Government of Orissa proposed to take up Upper Kolab Multi-purpose Project as quickly as possible.

It has been shown by different studies that most of the time the development projects are set up in the underdeveloped areas where the development and political costs are low. The Koraput district is full of natural resources on the one hand and populated by the tribals in majority who are weak—socially, politically and economically. The topography resources and the marginality of local people socially, economically and politically provided a suitable situation for the strong power lobby.

The lack of awareness, illiteracy, absence of any contact with the outside world made the tribals in Koraput socio-politically weak. The isolation maintained by the Britishers and the feudal rulers for their self-interests continued after the abolition of the feudal system. The people were kept away from the knowledge and information about the development planning in Upper Kolab. They were not aware of the planning of this project till they were called to the dam site for a public gathering on the day of laying foundation stone of the project by Smt. Nandini Satapathy, the then Chief Minister of Orissa. Only a few members of Scheduled Castes who used to visit nearby markets had heard the rumour about the project. Otherwise, nobody came to the villages and informed about the proposal of this project. The people remembered only the meeting on the day of laying foundation stone which gave information about the plan of the construction of a dam there. The socio-economic and political factors and the ignorance of the people made it obvious that the cost of development of the project in terms of acquisition of land, displacement, compensation and rehabilitation was going to be less expensive. The lack of political awareness among the people gave least chance for any resistance to stop the project.

Cost-Benefit Analysis of the Project

The multipurpose project of Upper Kolab got approved by the authority primarily for the production of hydro-electricity and creating irrigation potential in the Jeypore plateau of the district. The project envisaged the maximum utilisation of water resources for generation of 90 MW of firm power with the installed capacity of 240 MW (80 MW x 3). The installed capacity was increased later by adding another unit i.e. 80 MW x 4. The estimate of creating irrigation potential was 44544 hectare of land. Besides these primary objectives, possibility of supplying the water of Jeypore Municipality was kept open. It was expected to be completed within seven years of construction and the first unit of power project was to be installed in the year 1982. The benefit cost ratio was estimated to be 4.40 at 10 per cent interest. (Irrigation and Power Department, 1972)

The construction of dam was to submerge valuable cultivable land, village forests and displace the people from their villages. Many public works like roads, bridges, water works, transmission lines were also to be affected. It required the acquisition of private as well as government land and pay compensation to the affected people and agencies. The displaced people had to be resettled and rehabilitated by the project authority. It was proposed to reclaim the land in the command area of the project and develop them with the modern facilities and amenities for the rehabilitation of the people.

The overestimation of the benefit and the under estimation of the cost of the project has been observed in the proposal of Upper Kolab Multi-purpose Project like Rengali or most of other projects. The construction of different aspects of the project could not go along the construction plan. The different reasons for slip age in the construction programme are given in the *History of Upper Kolab Project,* Vol. 1 (1988) as the following:

(i) over ambitious construction programme,
(ii) delay in infrastructure development works,
(iii) unworkable construction targets,
(iv) delay in mobilisation by M/s H.C.C. Ltd.,
(v) natural calamities,
(vi) delay in rehabilitation work,
(vii) foundation problems,
(viii) slow progress of masonary works,
(ix) slow progress of gate erection works,
(x) delay in finalisation of tenders.

Besides these, there are other factors also mentioned which affected the progress of works such as non-availability of construction materials, and spare parts, inadequate powers of field staff, ineffectively of staff. Similarly the other construction works also got delayed due to various reasons.

The delay in construction of main dam works delayed the other aspects of the project. The construction was started in 1976 and was completed in 1998 through some of the minor work went upto 1991-92. The first unit of power production could not be installed though it was planned to be installed capacity. The government source shows that during the year 1993-94, the percentage of firm power to installed capacity of the Upper Kolab Project was only 26.69% (Directorate of Economics and Statistics, 1995, Table 9.2)

At the time of field work of this study (1994), only three units were in functioning condition. One of the officials of the Power Plant Division– II of the Upper Kolab Project said that all the four units were never in working condition. The power generating machines procured from the indigenous market were not good in quality. Most of the time, there was some technical problem or the other and, that affected the production of firm power.

The irrigation project is still under construction. The Satiguda Dam is already constructed but the distributory system viz. Jeypore Main Canal and Padampur distributory work is in progress. It is expected to be completed by 1998 which was started in 1976. The construction of the dam and power project was financed by the State government aided by the Central Government. The irrigation project was financed by the state in the initial stage. The construction of Jeypore main canal from 14 km. to 42 km. is being aided by the OECF (Overseas Economic Cooperation Fund) Japan with the aid of 3769 million Japan Yen. The irrigation started in the VIIth Plan (1985-90). In the annual plan of 1991-92, the potential could be achieved with 7000 and 5250 hectares of irrigation in Kharif and Rabi crop respectively (Dalua, 1991, Table 6.01).

The underestimation of the cost and not considering the cost of many of the aspects of the project has led to the overrun of time and the cost. The latest revised cost of the project in 1987 estimated the total cost of the project to Rs. 9362.28 lakhs from the original estimate of Rs. 1517.27 lakhs in 1972 (Irrigation and Power Dept, 1988, Table – 9-26/1). It is a 617.04 per cent overrun of the cost from the original estimate. The Table 9-26/1 of the History of Upper Kolab Project (1988) and the Revised Estimate – 1976, Upper Kolab Project (1980) give the estimates of the project with its reasons. The comparison between the original and the latest estimate of some of the project head shows significant differences.

Table 6
Comparison Between the Original Estimate and the Revised of 1987 in Rupees (Lakh)

Heads	3rd revised estimate	4th revised estimate	Difference
Land (Reservoir)	321.98	2946.00	2642.02
Works (Main dam and ancillaries)	855.19	4247.45	3392.26
Establishment	108.66	838.70	730.04
Miscellaneous	58.50	526.19	467.69

Source: Irrigation & Power Department, 1988, Vol. 1, Table-9 26/1.

The cost of establishment and miscellaneous increased because of the inadequate provision in those heads of the project. Some of the principal reason for excess cost in works were such a higher rate of execution, rise in the cost of construction materials, provisions of new workers, changes in the work plan. In case of land, the cost increased due to the land acquisition, compensation, rehabilitation and soil conservation. There was no proper speculation over the cost of different aspects of the project. The lack of proper planning and ignoring the human and environmental aspects led to overrun in the estimate of the project cost. Some of the examples can be cited here. There was increase in the cost of relocation of communication from the original provision of Rs. 45.72 lakh to Rs. 556.00 lakh in the cost of acquisition of land and rehabilitation of the displaced people from the original estimate of Rs. 13.20 lakhs to Rs. 477.00 lakhs in the revised estimate of 1979 (Irrigation and Power Dept., 1980: 8-10). *The History of Upper Kolab Project* (1988) states that if actually the rehabilitation works were time consuming the same could have been reflected properly in the construction programme without huge additional expenditure in procurement of lower cranes and other machines which were not all that necessary.

It was in reflection an optimistic planning of construction programme of the project. Even though the irrigation project is yet to be completed, with the over estimate of the benefits and under estimate of the costs, the Upper Kolab Project may also not be cost effective. The cost overrun of more than 600 per cent from its original estimate excluding the cost of irrigation distributory system which is in progress is definitely going to reduce the cost benefit ratio of the Upper Kolab Multipurpose Project.

Resettlement and Rehabilitation Measure in the Upper Kolab Project

The land acquisition and the Resettlement and Rehabilitation measures were administered under the control of Revenue Divisional Commissioner, Southern Division, Berhampur. The office of the Special Land Acquisition and Resettlement and Rehabilitation was established in Koraput, to look after the acquisition of land along with the Resettlement and Rehabilitation of the displaced people. The tahsildars of Koraput, Boriguna and Kotpad were empowered as zone officers. The acquisition of land, the Resettlement and Rehabilitation of the displaced people took place within Koraput district. It involved less administrative machinery, unlike, in the case of the Rengali Dam Project. A Rehabilitation Advisory Committee was constituted including official and non-official members, to coordinate and supervise the Resettlement and Rehabilitation programmes.

Land Acquisition

Initially, it was estimated about 6400 families were to be affected by the Upper Kolab Project in 147 villages. During the monsoon of 1987, the reservoir level rose from EL 845.00 to EL 856.00 m., which was 2 mts. below the FRL. Even at this level, some families were affected who were initially not supposed to be affected. Similarly more land than initially expected were submerged in some village. So some mistakes are observed in the FRL, marking. As soon as this mistake was found, a fresh survey was undertaken to identify the correct position. Therefore, there is no consitency in the data available from different sources. The government data also do not show consistency on some aspects.

The Land Acquisition and Resettlement and Rehabilitation authorities and the Office of the Chief Engineer, Upper Kolab, give the information at the time of field work (1994) that 3180 families were displaced from 53 villages, which were affected fully and partly. However, there are different views on this by different authorities.

Due to the wrong marking of villages to be affected at FRL, the original estimate of land to be submerged proved wrong. The latest data available from the Office of the Chief Engineer about the Upper Kolab Project show that the project acquired 31234 acres of land. This consisted of:

a.	Private land	24476.49	acres
b.	Government land	6567.9	acres
c.	Forest land	189.95	acres
	Total =	31234.34	acres

Besides this, the Upper Kolab Project submerged public properties like major district roads at different places, National Highway No. 48, Jawahar Water Works Sunabeda, Koraput Water Works, High Voltage transmission line of OSEB, properties of Central Cattle Breeding Farm and Orissa Small Industries Corporation, Sunabeda.

Apart from the land acquired for the reservoir, and other establishments, land were reclaimed by the project for the Resettlement and Rehabilitation of the displaced people from different sources—

a.)	Batasna and Nuagaon circles in 23 villages in Kotpad Tahsil	9432.00 acres
b.)	Boriguma Civil circle in 25 villages of Boriguma Tahsil	3268.00 acres
	Total	2700.00 acres

Source: Irrigation and Power Department, 1988: 575-576

The villages were submerged in different phases along with the rise in the water level in the reservoir. The following table shows the population affected in different phases:

The first phase of displacement took place in June 1984, when the reservoir level rose upto 835 mt. The second phase of displacement took place in June-July 1985, when the RL rose upto 850 mt. The third phase took place with the evacuation of one group of villages in June 1985 and another group of villages in June 1987 with the RL of 856 mt. The fourth phase of displacement took place in June 1988, when the RL rose up reaches 858 mt. After the displacement of the villages in different phases, a group of 104 families got displaced in two villages in 1990, after a resurvey in June 1989, whereas some of the families were displaced (Dalua, 1993, Annexure III, GOO, 1988 Tables 5/4, 5/6). There is no information available about the extent of submergence of 57 villages where the families were displaced. The Land Acquisition and Resettlement and Rehabilitation Office and the Chief Engineer Office, UPK, gave the information about 53 villages among which, 26 villages were fully and 27 villages were partly submerged thus displacing the inhabitants. Due to mistakes in the marking of villages, which are to submerged, the displacement process continued from 1984 to 1990.

Table 7

Population Displaced in Phases

Phase	No. of villages affected	No. of families displaced			Total families	Total population displaced
		SC	ST	Gen		
1st	5	129	431	135	695	3058
2nd	21	163	569	678	1410	6422
3rd	23*	90	375	323	788	3550
4th	9*	15	27	52	94	448
5th	2*	-	4	100	104	516
Satiguda pond	2*	45	15	20	80	411
Total	62	442	1421	1308	3171	14105
%		13.94	44.82	41.25	100	

* 2 + 1 + 2=5 are repeat villages

Source: Dalua A.K., 1993: 162

The land for the Upper Kolab Project was acquired through the guidelines of the Land Acquisition Act, 1894 like in the Rengali Dam Project. The procedure of giving compensation for the land acquired, the tree, houses, well was the same as followed in the Rengali Dam Project. It was decided that the rehabilitation policy announced for the Rengali project should be followed for rehabilitation of the affected families of Upper Kolab Project by the D.O.No. 16043, Irr. 1 (p) (R)- 4/79, dated 1-5-1979 (Dalua, 1991: 25-26). The displaced people of the Rengali Project demanded further improvement in the Resettlement and Rehabilitation provisions which were incorporated by the government through different resolutions and amendments.

After the resolutions on the Resettlement and Rehabilitation policy of the Rengali Project, and before the completion of the displacement and Resettlement and Rehabilitation process in UKP– several new resolutions were passed for the Resettlement and Rehabilitation of the project affected people, of different water resources projects. But they were not made applicable to Upper Kolab Project. The existing Resettlement and Rehabilitation policy for this project was to provide six acres of unirrigated or three acres of irrigated land along with 0.50 acre for the homestead. The cash grants for these provisions was Rs. 14040. In course of time, it was modified in 1989 and was made as five acres of unirrigated 250 irrigated land with the 0.50 acre for the homestead or Rs. 178875 as cash grant (G.O. Resolution No. Irr. UIP 25/88-240, dated 3-1-89). Later, it was further amended in 28 August 1989, GO resolution No. 36842 to Rs. 20075 as cash grant. It was amended again in 1990. The displacement and Resettlement and Rehabilitation process was not over till 1990, due to mistake in the making of submergence levels. The Resettlement and Rehabilitation provision approved in the year 1989 could have been applied in the last phase, if not the approved provision of the year 1990. Similarly, the definition of the family to be entitled for receiving Resettlement and

* *The LA and Resettlement and Rehabilitation office gave the data that 526 out of 3180 families resettled in the colonies and hence rest 2654 families took cash grant.*

Rehabilitation provisions, enhancement of cash compensation were approved when the Resettlement and Rehabilitation process was in progress. Some families, particularly the 104 families that got displaced after the 1990, got the benefits of the new provisions, which were not applied for everyone in the Upper Kolab Project.

Marooned Villages

There were many villages located at higher contours which were affected indirectly by the reservoir. In the case of some villages, the people lost most of their cultivated land, which got submerged in the reservoir. In some other cases, the villages were surrounded by water either on two or three sides and this cut off their communication links with other villages or market centres. There was no Resettlement and Rehabilitation provision for such villages, except compensation for the loss of the land. The Rehabilitation Advisory Committee suggested the construction of roads wherever it was possible, and if the road construction would cost more than the cost of resettlement and rehabilitation cost then the people would be resettled. The village Parajapondi was provided with the Resettlement and Rehabilitation provisions when the reservoir surrounded it on three sides. There was no record available about the number of marooned villages. The officials from L.A. and Resettlement and Rehabilitation office said that there were many villages marooned like this. The Koraput District General Secretary of Akhil Bhartiya Adivasi Vikas Parishad who visited many of the marooned villages gave a list of sixteen of these villages.

For the villages, where road construction was not possible, boats were to be plied for providing communication link to outside villages. For maintaining the ferry ghats and ferries, the Upper Kolab Project was to pay Rs. 1,10, 000 for each ghat. The ferries were to run by the Gram Panchayats.

Mode of Resettlement and Rehabilitation

Land for land was the basic guiding principle for the resettlement and rehabilitation of the displaced people of the

Upper Kolab Project. The landless people were also provided this Resettlement and Rehabilitation provision. As per the provision in the Rengali Dam Project, each displaced family was supposed to be given six acres of unirrigated or three acres of irrigated land with 0.50 acres of homestead. The same time, it was kept open to take part cash land provisions in the resettlement colonies or opt for full cash grant in lieu of land and resettle anywhere they liked.

There were seven resettlement colonies reclaimed by the project in Bariguma and Kotpad Tahsils of Koraput district. The Dandakaranasa Development Authority, a Central Agency, undertook reclamation work in the resettlement colonies. During the period from May 1979 to June 1980, the reclamation of land was done only for 1318 acres only. The agency had to shift somewhere else, for which the reclamation of land was done for 73304.49 acres out of 9433.00 acres available (Dalua, 1993: Table 5.3). The land available from different sources in Boriguma circle was not reclaimed, as the response from the displaced people to resettle there was negative.

Among the displaced families, 528 of them resettled in the government sponsored colonies with either part land cash or fully land, benefits in different colonies, and hence 2743 of them took full cash benefits and resettled on their own (Dalua, 1993, Annexure-III*). Keeping in view of the inexperience of the tribals with the larger amounts of cash and the possibility of expenditure on drinking and other unproductive conspicuous consumption, the Rehabilitation Advisory Committee made the following decisions as not to pay the entire rehabilitation grant of Rs. 14,040.00 in cash at once.

Deposit in six yearly National Savings Certificate	Rs. 6,000.00
Deposit in five yearly fixed deposit	Rs. 6,000.00
Deposit in Savings account	Rs. 1,500.00
Cash Payment	Rs. 540.00
Total	**Rs. 14,040.00**

This arrangement was implemented with the approval of the Revenue Divisional Commissioner (Southern division). The condition was put that the money could be taken out from the deposits only when the displaced person justified the withdrawal to the authority about the necessity of money, with an affidavit in the court.

Extent of Resettlement and Rehabilitation

The seven-resettlement colonies were allotted 9425.00 acres of land for the purpose of homestead, agricultural land, common land. The colonies were provided with other infrastructural facilities to resettlement 2072 displaced families. The following table gives the number of families form different choice with background in different resettlement colonies.

The table indicates that 526 families out of 3180 displaced families resettled in four out of seven colonies. Among the resettled families, 5.70% of them were SCs, 37.8% of them were STs and 56.5% of them were other castes. But only 17% (526) of the total displaced families (3180) and 25% of the total families to be resettled (2072) decided to resettle in the government colonies. The remaining families took cash grant, and resettled on their own at different places. There was no information available about their whereabouts.

Table 8

No. of Families Resettled in Different Colonies

No. of Colony	No. of families resettled/displaced			Total
	SC	ST	Others	
1, 2 & 3	0	0	0	0 4
21	198	43	262	
5	3	0	54	57
6	0	0	76	76
7	6	1	124	131
Total	30/442	199/1421	297/1317	526/3180
%	(5.70)	(37.80)	(56.5)	(100.00)

Source: Land Acquisition and Resettlement and Rehabilitation Office, Koraput, at the time of Field work in 1994.

Neither the project nor the government had taken any satisfactory steps to provide communication facilities to the marooned villages. The boats were not adequate. The villagers had to use locally made wooden boats individually, or in groups, and cross the reservoir to reach the outside world. They were cut and isolated from all governmental programmes.

The resettlement colonies were constructed with different infrastructure facilities, before the displaced people were shifted there. The History of Upper Kolab Project (1988) gives the details of colony-wise rehabilitation works proposed and done. The information available from the land acquisition and Resettlement and Rehabilitation office and the Chief Engineer office, Upper Kolab Project, are compiled below:

Cost of Resettlement and Rehabilitation

The cost overrun occurred from the original estimate on Resettlement and Rehabilitation of the displaced people and compensation for the other affected people due to various reasons as mentioned earlier. The revision of expenditures on different sub-heads on Resettlement and Rehabilitation were recommended and approved from time to time. The information available from the study by Dalua (1993) and Irrigation and Power Department (1988) did not seem to be latest, regarding the expenditure. The available information from the office of the Chief Engineer, Upper Kolab Project, at the time of the field work of this study, 1994, it was found that Rs. 3,93,94,3445 was paid as cash grant for the self-rehabilitated people and Rs. 1,25,78,780 was spent on reclamation of the resettlement colonies. However, Dalua (1993) gives the details of the expenditure of different sub-heads till 1987.

In the Upper Kolab Project, the affected people had relatively egalitarian society. Except a few general caste people, the tribals and scheduled castes had shared the similar socio-economic situation. The other castes namely Malis and Ronas were the farming class who used to grow vegetable and other cash crops. They were economically better than the other villages though they did not gain much respect socially in the village. They were used to the cash economy and had relatives in different market centres. Most of this caste groups opted for cash R&R provisions and resettled individually by buying lands at their relatives place. The affected people from the villages Koronga and Prajapondi, felt that the Malis and the Ronas (most of whom opted for cash grants) were the gainers from the project. But the colonywise distribution of colony dwellers shows that except colony 4, other colonies (Nos. 5, 6, 7) were resettled mostly by the other caste people. The District General Secretary of Akhil Bhartiya Adivasi Vikas Parishad who happened to be a tribal from the same district, also said that the Malis, Ronas, Paikas (General Caste) were the gainer from the project. They were basically cultivators from the plain areas who migrated to this hilly areas long time back. They were engaged in cultivation activities on the plain land, which was not the case with the tribals and scheduled caste people.

Table 9
Infrastructural Facilities

Facilities	Nos. in	R & R	Colonies		Total
	4	5	6	7	
Roads	N.A.	N.A.	N.A	N.A.	76 kms.
School buildings	2	1	1	1	5
Open wells	6	3	3	2	14
Tube wells	4	2	5	4	15
Tank/Pond	2	1	1	2	6

In the case of the Upper Kolab Project, the tribals and Scheduled Castes used to practise shifting cultivation since ages. It was considered as encroachment of forest land and were not considered for the payment of compensation. Their traditional mode of production was not accepted by the modern economy. Secondly, whatever compensation or cash grants of R & R provisions they got, they neither could enjoy the money by themselves nor did they use it for any productive purposes. Due to their illiteracy and inexperience of handling cash, the major amount of cash benefits were put in the saving accounts which could be withdrawn through an affidavit in the court. The advocates exploited the illiteracy and inexperience of the affected people in managing their accounts. Thirdly, the PAPs who opted for individual resettlement by taking cash grants were not assisted by the project to resettle in anyway unlike the individual resettlers, in the Rengali Dam Project. There was no record or information about these individual resettler. The condition of the individual resettlers of the Koronga village around the project site looks miserable.

Nearly, those who were resettled in the government sponsored colonies, were promised good land with the irrigation. A senior government officials from the Irrigation Department of state government who was closely associated with the implementation of the Upper Kolab Project himself says:

"Government spent a lot of money on reclaiming the land identified for the resettlers. But reclamation has not been done properly. Tree stumps were not uprooted and for which at several places tree growth has again appeared. The land selected is dominated by laterite soils of low fertility, yield and, therefore not encouraging (Dalua, 1993: 182)".

The shifting cultivators were compelled to adopt the plain land cultivation, that too in infertile land, and without canal water as promised in the R & R provisions, even after five years of resettlement. Besides this, the absence of forest made them deprived of their ages old forest based economy, and other usages of forest produces in their daily life. Therefore, it was not surprising to know that many households from colony no. 4 went back to their old village, Parajapondi inspite of having many problems there.

There were some specific groups of people who suffered due to the displacement irrespective of the caste and phase of displacement namely the women, widows and son/brother married after the reference date of family enumeration. Except, higher caste (Brahmin, Chasa, Paika, Gudia, Karanas) women, the other women used to participate in the economics as well as domestic activities of the household before displacement. The loss of forest decline in household and village agriculture worsened their participation in collecting firewood and agricultural activities. The process of displacement and R & R involved some labour intensive activities like building house in the resettlement village developing the agricultural land, visiting R & R offices regarding their problems. The widows with the young children faced problem to decide and do according to their wishes since they could not do preparatory activities by themselves. They followed the other villagers but they had to depend on others for these activities. All the families were going through the same situation and they all were busy in making arrangements for their own household first. They helped others including the widows only after finishing their work. Even for the ploughing of land in each agricultural season, people come after finishing their work. Due to the dependence on others, the widows could not do their agricultural work and other labour intensive activities on time.

The participation of women among the PAPs of the Upper Kolab Project had a greater role in the household economy. They had equal participation in the collection and production of food along with their male counterparts. Starting from the cleaning of the agricultural land on hill slopes, sowing the grains, weeding, harvesting, and thrashing, to cooking and feeding food to the family members and collecting different forest produces to supplement their food stock, the women had always participated actively. The displacement from their native villages also displaced them from their role in the household economy. In the Government colonies, the people had to cultivate plain land. While cultivating plain land, it has to be ploughed by the bullocks or buffaloes, which is done only by the males. The women could not do ploughing but used to hew the hill slopes through their traditional harvesting instruments. Secondly, they cannot supplement the household food by the forest produces like fruits, roots, leaves, and flower due to the absence of forest.

Conclusion

The large dams create irrigation potential and hydro-electricity for nation. But the picture on the extent of creation and utilization raises questions on the cost-benefit and class-benefit analysis. Despite the unsatisfactory performance of these projects, more and more projects are proposed. The people paying price for these projects are far away from sharing the development benefits of these modern temples of India. Moreover due to the poor and intensive resettlement and rehabilitation measures of the project authorities, the project affected persons in general and the vulnerable groups like tribals, dalits, women, service castes are put at risk of impoverishment. All these projects seems to an outcome of the struggle between two interest groups - the powerful ruling class and the powerless/weaker sections who are ruled. Even, in the resettlement and rehabilitation, the people having better support system cope with the situation better than who have poor or not support system.

REFERENCES

1. Central Water Commission:(1990), *National Register of Large Dams,* New Delhi, Govt. of India.
2. Central Board of Irrigation and Power (1989) *Modern Temples of India* New Delhi, Govt.of India.
3. CMIE(1992), *Basic Statistics Relating to Indian Economy,* Bombay, CMIE.
4. CMIE Relating (1994), Economy Intelligence Service Basic Statistics, State of India, Bombay, CMIE
5. CMIE (1995), *Economic Intelligence Service,* India's Agricultural Sector, A Compendium of Statistics Bombay, CMIE
6. Dalaua, A.K. 1991, *Irrigation in Orissa,* Cuttack, water and Land Management Institute.
7. Dalaua, A.K. 1993, *Environmental Impact of Large Reservoir Projects on Human Settlements,* New Delhi, Ashish Publishing House.
8. Directorate of Economics and Statistics 1990-91, *District Statistical Hand Book,* Koraput, Bhubaneswar Govt. of Orissa.
9. Directorate of Economics and Statistics 1995, *Economic Survey 1994-95,* Bhubaneswar, Govt. of Orissa.
10. Irrigation and Power Dept. (1972), *Upper Kolab Dam Project,* Project Report, Vol.1, General Vol.1, General Report. Govt. of Orissa.

11. Irrigation and Power Dept. (1988), *History of Upper Kolab Project*, Vol.1, Govt. Orissa.
12. Irrigation and Power Dept. (1980), *Upper Kolab Multipurpose Project* (Power Development Only), revised Estimate of 1976, Govt. of Orissa.
13. Mahapatra L.K. (1994), *Development Project and Rehabilitation of the Displaced Persons.* Paper Presented in the Seminar at Institute for Socio-Economic Development Bhubaneshwar.
14. Mahaptra P.C (1988), The Strategic Deficiency of Tribal Development District. In *Adibasi*, Vol. Xxviii, No.I March.
15. Mahapatra L.K.(1989), Rehabilitation of Tribals affected by Major Dams and other projects in Orissa, in A report on the Workshop On Rehabilitation of persons Displaced by Development Projects, A.P., Fernandez (ed.) Banglore, Institute for Social and Economic Change and MYRADA.
16. Patnaik, N. 1988, *Tribes of Koraput District, in Adibasi*, Vol. XXVIII, No.1, pp. 1-18.
17. Pattanaik, S, Mishra, Das (1987), Hirakud Dam Project, Expectations and Realities, in *People and Dams*, New Delhi. PRIA.
18. Stanley, W 1996, Machkund, Upper Kolab and NALCO Projects in Koraput District, Orissa, *Economic and Political Weekly*, June.

2

Impact of Development Induced Displacement on Tribals

— *Dr. S. N. Tripathy**

Out of numerous problems manifested in recent years, the problem of 'development induced displacement' is one of the deep concerns in our country. Large number of people are constrained to displace in the wake of river dam projects, defence establishment, mining activities and industrial undertakings etc. proper utilisation of land and other resources are indispensable for economic development of any region but at the same time conflicting consideration of their impact on original habitants, ecological system and lives of displaced people are equally significant.

Development Induced Development

The available statistical data demonstrates that during 1951-1990 about 213 lakh of people were displaced because of development project and out of which about 40 per cent were tribals (Fernandes, 1994).[1] In this paper an effort has been made to focus the impact of development induced displacement people in general and tribal people in particular.

Needless to mention that tribals in India constitute about 8 per cent of the total population and rank second in terms of total numbers in the world, next to Africa.

A number of commissions and committees were appointed

* *Post-Doctoral Research Fellow, Deptt. of Economics, Aska Science College, Orissa-761111*

from time to time look into the problems of development in tribals regions of the country. These commissions suggested measures to remove the socio-economic imbalances and breakdown the psychological barrier which prevailed in the tribal pockets. But ironically, it has been observed that whenever river dam projects or industrialization process is embarked upon, the worst victims are tribals, —who constitute significant segment of the total population of the project area. To illustrate more vividly we can analyse the development project induced displacement.

The Bargi dam project was completed in 1980 on the river Narmada with 10 times more expenditure of the original estimated budget. While 101 villages were annihilated due to the dam, 160 villages were submerged with water. An aggregate of 1,14,000 people were became homeless.[2] Due to construction of Sardar Sarovar Project dam 37000 hectors of land will be submerged and 3.2 lakhs of people will be displaced.[3] So far 41,450 families have been displaced but there has been no systematic plans or rehabilitation policy for these families even after 14 years of their displacement.[4]

There were 22,148 families displaced due to Subarnrekha dam project. Even after 43 years of its construction, only 50 per cent of the displaced families have been rehabilitated and provided compensation.[5]

There is a plan to construct dams in Deogam of Bargarh District, Keutapalli of Subarnapur District and Godhoneswar of Boudh District for production of 300 mtr electricity output, resulting in displacement of population inhabitated in 57 villages. The main purpose of these dams construction is to project and safeguard the adjoining villages of Hirakud dam which further confirms that Hirkud Dam poses a great danger. Again, there is a proposal for construction of 5 dams by Chatisgarh Government over Mahanadi river. If it is materialised, there is an apprehension that the water level will significantly decline during summer. Moreover, possibility of occurrence of frequent floods in rainy season can not be avoided.[6]

Because of Tehri dam project 9,000 families in 37 villages will be displaced. In Upper Kolab 22000 families are to be displaced in aggregate out of which 70% are tribals and scheduled castes. Twenty- two villages are worst hit due to such a dam project. The Baghalati dam project though started since 1988, has not yet been completed. The original outlay of Rs. 4,544 lakhs have increased to Rs. 6,711 lakhs and by the time of its completion the expenditure may be doubled. The original estimation of irrigation capacity was 6,050 hectors which is now told to be 1,650 hectors.[7]

The displaced people of 6 villages in Gajapati District due to Harabhangi dam project have not been provided compensation so far.

The original outlay was Rs. 14.81 crores in Potteru Irrigation dam project, started in 1973 and completed in 1988, increased to 148.07 crores. Again, due to low quality of work and misappropriation of funds, the outlets are filled up by mud which obstructed the irrigation to the desired destinations. Moreover, 45.9% of the electricity produced because of these dams have been used by leakage and illegal uses.[8]

Adverse Impact on Displaced Tribals

Though such dams are constructed at the cost of displaced population originally inhabited in interior regions, forest areas but they have been deprived of the benefits.

It has been observed by the researcher that displacement of tribals in project area cause untold misery as the life supporting system of the tribals the common property resources land, forests etc. are snatched away from the tribals by the politicians, engineers and contractorss. Most of tribals' lands are cultivated as decided by villages chief through community farming. The simple, illiterate, poverty striken tribals do not know the entitlement of land or 'Pattas'. The procedure of getting land right or 'Patta' is so difficult that a tribal farmer can not get it so easily. Moreover, the Mahajans, businessmen, traders advance loans to needy, poverty–striken tribals in the mortgage of their land. Ultimately, land alienation takes place in tribals areas. Though the tribals cultivate the land but the 'Patta' (registered land deed) remains with the non-tribals mostly the traders, contractors. Thus, due to development project a lion's share is taken by non-tribals. Moreover, the programmes of development in the tribals regions have taken into account the wide range of constrains such as wide-spread poverty, under-developed infrastructure, neglect of employment needs, high illiteracy, lack of infrastructural facilities and limited geographical coverage.

Ironically, as has been observed (Tripathi, 2000) that investment in tribal areas for the provision of infrastructure like roads, building, electricity and opening of the tribal regions through mining, industrial development and river dam projects instead of reducing the process of exploitation has aggravated the problem and widen the gap of inequality.[9] Thus, all such investments and development efforts posed major problems like displacement of tribals from their original inhabitations and exposure to exploitation by external agents of traders, moneylenders and contractors.[10]

Notwithstanding clear directions under the Constitution of India (Article 46) that prevention and elimination of exploitation should be ensured and socio-economic development should be accelerated, it could not be possible for the central and state Government to halt exploitation mainly in the sphere of land alienation, indebtedness, exploitation by middlemen and traders.[11]

Resettlement of Tribals

Resettlement is a process of re-establishing the homes, livelihood, cultural and social relations, institutions and value system of the displaced families aiming at developing a new and stable community life style in the altered environment. Rehabilitation is a more comprehensive term which devotes a long-term generation and re-establishment of the socio-economic and cultural life of the people.[12] Thus, it is the uprooting and dismemberment of the social, moral and economic web of life built over generations. There have been cases of brutality and repression as in the case of Hirakud oustees in Orissa when they resisted evaluation. They were finally loaded like cattle in trucks and some seven died falling from them. Displaced people suffer great deprivation more particularly children.

The impoverishment risks of landlessness, marginalisation joblessness and social disintegration affecting displaced people in general as well as affects the children.[13]

In spite of adequate provisions in the Articles 164, 244, 244(A), 278, 330, 332, 334, 335, 338, 342 and fifth and sixth schedules of the constitution aiming of development and protection of interest of tribals, the powerful exgenious forces of moneylenders, contractors, officials having their link with political personnel and police could exert dominant control and gratify the selfish greed of exploiting tribals. The poverty stricken, illiterate, innocent, simple tribals fail to withstand the conunterveiling exgenious forces and becoming prey to all types of exploitation.

Obviously, the World Commission on Dams (WCD) focuses the lack of legal framework, political will and planning infrastructure to mitigate and redress the substantial negative effects that large dam have on environment and society. The report also adds that the dams cater to the well to do. 62% of the population displaced is that of tribals. Even the electricity and irrigation benefits routimely by pass the 'Project' attested persons and are disproportionately consumed by the landed framers and urban electricity consumers. Even the distribution of most of the cases and benefits of the large dams seem to accentuate socio-economic inequalities. It further states that the marginal contribution of large dams to increased foodgrains production (in India) is less than 19%.

Conclusion

In this context it is imperative to suggest that proper information and greater sensitivity are needed to deal with the problems of displaced and more particularly the 'adivasis' or tribals. The *Sunday Express* (2000) aptly pointed out: "Sustainable development is not just so much surgon, and rehabilitating those who are uprooted by project that has very little to do with their lives has now come to be recognised as an in-built features of every blue print. These days, it's cool to care and to be seen as caring."

It's ironic and tragic that a movement that has contributed to this consensus in developmental discourse has got little in return. The other out-of-the courtroom verdict that was almost as soon as the Supreme Court gave its ruling is that the movement has lost the ground beneath its feet, that the activists should either put-up with an ever growing down or just leave. It's an epitaph the NBA didn't choose, and one they'll fight in typical fashion. It's a question of who blinks first."[14]

It is equally pertinent to quote:

"There is a need to strongly support a hidden cause of a similar nature that to beyond the Narmada Project. Of the 300 million plus population in our towns and cities, perhaps 100 million live in slums and footpaths. Most of them are ousted from their home in rural areas for want of opportunities to earn a modest livelihood. What kind of development have we persued in the past 43 years, if these citizens of India are condemned to a sub-human excellence? We need a major grass–roots efforts to turn around the misplaced priorities of our past and present policies. There is much bigger deem called India's distorted development displacing millions of people each year which unfortunately gets no attention either from activists in the country or the urban intelligentsia whose voices are heard within India and abroad".[15]

The analysis brought to light that in tribal regions the dam projects could not help the tribals. The unskilled, illiterate and simple tribals ate victimised and thus, developmental projects have detrimental impact on tribals.

Non-recognition of rights over resources and restrictions on their use, alienation of tribals from the means of production, denial of due entitlement of labour, distressed payments of wages and misappropriation of funds, thus, leakages of investible resources in tribal regions have kept the tribals in the web of misery and stagnation. In tribal dominated state in India, the life supporting system of the local tribals have been snatched away by non-tribals and state institutions. As a result of which, tribal movement have originated in fierce struggle for the rights.[16]

REFERENCES

1. Fernades, Walter (1994), *Development Induced Displacement in the Tribal Areas of Eastern India,* A Research Project Sponsored by the Indian Council of Social Science Research, New Delhi, Indian Social Institute, p. 24.
2. *The Pragatibadi* (The Oriya Daily), December, 27th , 2000, p. 4.
3. *The Anupum Bharat* (The Oriya Daily) 6th January, 2001, p. 5.
4. *Ibid.*
5. *Ibid.*
6. *Ibid.*
7. *Ibid.*
8. *Ibid.*
9. Tripathy, S.N. (2000) 'Co-operatives for Tribal Development', in Tripathy S. N. (Ed.) *Glimpses on Tribal Development,* Discovery Publishing House, New Delhi, p. 95.
10. *Ibid.*
11. Sen, Biswajit,' Impact of Tribal Welfare Programmes', *Yojana,* December 1-15, 1989, p. 9.
12. Alexius Ekka (1996), *Displacement and Children, My Name is Today,* Vol. IV, No. 3&4 July–December.
13. *Ibid.*
14. *The New S unday Express,* 29th October, 2000, p. 23
15. R.K. Pachauri (2000), *The Times of India* , November, 17th.
16. Tripathy, S. N. (2000), *Glimpses on Tribal Development,* Preface, op. cit.

3

Behavioural Concerns of the Displaced During Development

— *Dr. A. Ramakrishna**

Introduction

Those who are forced to leave their home areas or have to flee because of conflict, human rights violation, and other natural or human-made disasters are called internally displacement.

The most effective way to address displacement is to avoid conditions that might compel people to leave their homes against their will. When governments and other institutions respect human rights and humanitarian law, the likelihood of displacement is greatly reduced. But, In reality this is not the case. Displacement caused by large-scale development projects, such as dams or building schemes, can be considered arbitrary if they cannot be justified by overriding public interest. Even where such public interest established, those displaced by development projects should be consulted and compensated. The displacements must occur in a manner that does not violate other human rights and that minimizes the adverse effects of displacement.

Hence, the Guiding Principles emphasize that if displacement occurs, it should be temporary.

- Displacement should last not longer than required, by the compelling circumstances that legitimize the movements.

---

* *Asst. Professor, Institute of Advanced Study in Education, Osmania University, Hyderabad–500007.*

This means that solutions to displacement should be explored and implemented as soon as possible.

- Consultations with the populations to be displaced will identify some possible alternatives to displacement or they move voluntarily, if they understand the reasons that the movement is necessary and where they should relocate.
- Choices of relocation sites help protect rights and minimize disruption. They should permit the displaced to resume normal economic, social and other activities as quickly as possible.

Thus, a new definition of 'Development' should consider the aspects of development for whom, by whom, at what cost to the individual and the environment.

Development-induced displacement has overwhelmingly dominated the IDP scenario in India. Along side development-induced displacement new casual factors are fast emerging, namely,

- political causes, including secessionist movements
- identity-based autonomy movements
- localized violence
- environmental and development-induced displacement.

In order to achieve rapid economic growth, India has invested in industrial projects, dams, roads, mines, power plants and new cities which have been made possible only through massive acquisition of land and subsequent displacement of people.

The nature, frequency and extent of the causes of displacement in India vary. Total number of IDPs in India is 507,000 (The World Refugee Survey, Washington, 2000).

Whereas, Indian Social Institute has calculated total as 21.3 million, out of which the persons displaced due to dams are 16.4 –million, mines– 2.55 million, industrial development– 1.25 million and wild-life sanctuaries 7 national parks- 0.6 million.

'Natural' disaster-led displacement is never recorded after the initial dose of relied and rehabilitation assistance. One of the most serious aspects of the displacement belonging to this category has been the fact that the displacement has been silent but acute and frequent.

The displaced languish in camps where conditions are deficient. There is little healthcare, sanitation, or education. The authorities provide inadequate– if any–assistance. They have little hope for a long-term solution to their uprooted lives. The displaced are not simply a disadvantaged group or casualties of a natural disaster. They are victims of violence, persecution, and human rights abuse directed against them because of their membership in a particular group.

Crucially, government accountability for the consequences of state-imposed displacement has been virtually absent. While the states have aggressively clamoured for more benefits from development projects, they have consistently haggled over their share of rehabilitation costs and totally disregarded the plight of those displaced. The Draft National Policy for Rehabilitation is a multi-dimensional response to displacement with full rehabilitation and is still under consideration in Parliament. There is no international agency to deal with such types of displacement. There seems to be no immediate solution to IDP issues in India. Hence, community should take up self-help measures.

Significance

There is a need for planned interventions for restructuring the system in order to multiply such exceptions for vitalising public policies and programmes for better, quicker and more sustainable social and human development in the country.

The human development performance in the country in the last 50 years of Independence can only be rated as very low. Despite the Constitutional directives and Fundamental Rights and despite promises made repeatedly, the situation obtaining in the fields of elementary education, literacy, health care and employment and in such other basic areas has been rather pathetic and highly disappointing. The state and its various organs have thus failed even to discharge their minimum Constitutional obligations to the people.

The state agencies in India have been historically and even educationally conditioned to be insensitive to the needs of the lowly placed labouring people.

Under such conditions, human development would require not just some literacy and any casual work but inculcation of positive self-concepts and capability. They have to be helped to move away from dependent pawn-like behaviours to initiative and actor-like behaviours. Participation in organised collective action in people's movements as well as in self-initiated development action would greatly help in promoting and reinforcing such positive self-concepts. Public activism is also important for pressuring and activising the unwilling government to act for the welfare of the people and to decentralise and democratise the administration.

Creative and meaningful interaction between people and the state thus helps in releasing people-empowerment and democratisation in the wider society. As the assertive power of the people increases and as they become more and more concerned with social achievement goals, they would also activise the state for similar achievement goals, thus accelerating the process of democratic governance and sustainable human and economic development in the country.

Objectives of the Study

- To find out the behaviours that instill confidence and positive attitude towards displacement in view of the development.
- To develop activities which will ensure the attainment of the above behaviours in the people.

A comprehensive list of behaviours is developed through discussions with experts, research scholars and the people affected by the development projects. Basing over this, and review of related literature, a questionnaire was constructed 'to find out the behaviours that instill confidence and positive attitude towards displacement in view of the development'.

Development of behaviours is concerned with personality and hence, the individuals' personality and the way the self develops are considered.

'Self' is described in terms of the meanings for the individual that result from these ongoing processes (Prescott, 1957). The individual with favourable self-concept is a contributing member of the society, which in turn will enable him/her to face the critical situations. Further, the reactions of the individual in these situations depend on their emotions. So, the various emotions, which have a bearing either directly or indirectly, were taken up. For example, anxiety is shown as **'sharing'** while curiosity is expressed as **'alertness'**.

One-year-old child who will continue as **sharing** things or ideas as he makes entry into school indicates affection as **sympathy.**

Good personal and social **adjustments** developed by the end of second year lead to the development of favourable self-concept. This will in turn make the child to take **initiative** which is expressed as a **leadership** quality (Hurlock, 1994.).

By the time child is 4-5 years of age the personality pattern gets established. A few important personality traits that set during this period are: **courage, enthusiasm, cooperative, altruism** and **sympathy** (Hurlock, 1994).

The child, who does not need an immediate solution to all his problems and free to take a problem solving approach instead, is **spontaneous,** creative and original. If his social experience and relationships demean or isolate him, they produce strong emotions (such as enthusiasm) working for more satisfying roles and relationships. On the contrary, emotional identification (such as sympathy) permits more complex interpretations of the significance of the self and its roles in relation to objects, events and the persons.

An individual with favourable self-concept will be able to solve problems on his own without relying on others **(independent thinking)** He is free of some of the forces, which bear upon the child who feels inadequate.

Children are the most vulnerable section of the community. If they are unable to understand and rationalize the event, they may suffer from phobias, sleep disturbances, loss of interest in school work, and aggressive or undisciplined behaviour (the category most at risk are 8-12 years old). This is because the psychological processes involved in developing as a self include among others, reasoning.

The self-mediated, self-oriented processes continue to set new goals for experience, learning, role playing and inventing or creating and direct the behaviour of the individual toward their realization. He becomes dynamic and he initiates events to accomplish goals which he himself have set and lead others. Thus, when the child interacts with others, he may find himself organising and directing the group.

Though the behaviours are initiated during these childhood years, there is no guarantee that they exhibit them unless told to do so or imbibed by them through training. This can be achieved through involving them in various activities.

Activities

While developing the activities, the aspects borne in mind are indigenous material

- cost effectiveness
- user-friendliness
- comprehensibility and
- constituents of the behaviours.

The meanings of the behaviours are given below so that one can understand better while developing activities for them.

Adjustments– setting right the thing; putting in order the things, regulating the things; and making the things suitable or convenient for use.

Alertness– watchful; vigilant; nimble; and on the lookout against danger or attack.

Altruism– the unselfishness; and the principle of considering the well being and happiness of others first.

Cooperation– working together for a common purpose.

Courage– boldness; nerve oneself to a venture; courage to act upto what one believes or to be brave enough to do what one feels to be right; and the quality that enables a person to control fear in the face of danger or misfortune.

Enthusiasm– the strong feeling of admiration or interest.

Independent thinking– acting or thinking upon one's own lines; unwilling to be under obligation to others; not relying on others; and not depending on authority or control.

Initiative– the capacity to see what needs to be done and enterprise enough to do it; without being prompted by others; and be the first to take action.

Leadership– action of guiding or giving an example; give person a lead; encourage him by doing thing; and is in the lead.

Rationality– ability to reason.

Sharing– giving away part of; and enduring jointly with others during emergencies.

Spontaneity– a happening from natural impulse; and not caused or suggested by something or somebody outside.

Sympathy– capacity of being simultaneously affected with the same feeling as another; tendency to share another person's or thing's emotion or sensation or condition; and mental participation with another in his trouble or with another's trouble during the emergencies.

Activities are developed from the behaviours mentioned above in the following manner:

Altertness

Let the people discuss the weather. How many types of weather conditions can they describe? Ask them to prepare symbolic drawing of different weather conditions.

- clouds and shady sun – cloudy day
- bright sun with sunrays – sunny day
- cloud and water droplets – rainy day
- plant twig with leaves bent sideway – windy day.

Ask the people to make weather predictions each morning or during a meeting in a community hall and record them, were they right? If so, how many times each month? There could be right or wrong predictions and marked 'tick' or 'cross' in each corner of the symbolic drawings. Later ask them to compare their observations with the weather forecasts in the newspaper, radio and television broadcasts.

This activity enables the people to predict accurately over a period of time and prepare themselves to meet the eventualities from with it can be inferred that 'alertness' is developed.

Cooperation

People feel fun to have a community garden, which belongs to everybody. They grow radishes, green tail onions, lettuce, pumpkins, etc. Let a person get the seeds, the other sow them, still another water them. The people will feel proud and would check their plants many times a day. In this way, the people seek mutual help from each other to complete the task and from this it can be inferred that 'cooperation' is developed.

Sharing

During the occasions of festivals–religious or national, let the people assemble in a community hall and group into 5 members each. Then, they are allotted the work of keeping the surroundings clean. Group A members are asked to pick up small stones, bits of paper and other unwanted material from outside the hall. Group B members hold the broomstick and sweep the floor for cleaning. Next, group C members cut the colour papers, make different shapes and decorate the hall.

In this manner the people endure jointly the hardships and the fruits of work (it can also be a road laying, clean and green activities, etc). Thus, endurance in sharing with others is developed in the people.

Sympathy

Let people form pairs. One in each pair is blindfolded and each pair is asked to walk through a series of obstacles like a ditch, tree or an over hanging branch with the partner, who can see, leading. If obstacles are not available, these can be created with the marks on the ground, posting volunteers to be trees or using furniture (Joy of Learning—*Handbook of Environmental Education Activities*, 1986).

The partner who leads should do so without talking, by taking the hand of his blindfolded partner and make him feel the obstacles and difficulties the blind face in the daily life situations. This develops sympathetic feeling in the people. After a while, the roles can be exchanged.

Evaluation Procedures

The number of exposures required for the behaviour to be internalized varies from 5 to 10. The evaluation procedures are observation for alertness, cooperation and sharing and simulation for sympathy.

Similarly, the activities can be planned for other behaviours and their corresponding evaluation procedures.

Conclusions

Ability to manage displacement problems depends on the total personality of the individual. As it is very difficult and rather impractical to define personality, a set of behaviours, which enable the individual in particular and society in general to overcome displacement issues, is discussed. Therefore, it is natural that the list of behaviours in the present study is not exhaustive. Further, the activities developed are based on the perceptions of the researcher and review of related literature. It is therefore, to be stressed that the list of activities is illustrative and the activities may be modified and adopted to the local situations.

In this way and using these techniques, people can participate fully in the transition process, properly fulfil their obligations to society at large, and produce a generation of citizens whose outlook is sufficiently robust and enlightened to ensure that the earth survives and prospered in the 21st century and beyond.

REFERENCES

1. *Handbook for Applying the Guiding Principles on Internal Displacement*, Brookings Institution Project on Internal Displacement, Washington D.C., 1999.

2. Hurlock E.E (1994), *Child Growth and Development*, Fifth edition, Tata McGraw Hill Publishing Company Limited, New Delhi.
3. Joy of Learning – *Handbook of Environmental Education Activities*, Center for Environment Education, Ahmedabad, 1986.
4. Kumar, J.D. "Rights of Internally Displaced Persons in the Light of the Guiding Principles of Internal Displacement" paper presented at the seminar on Internally Displaced Persons in Ecumenical Christian Center, Bangalore during 22-24 September 2000.
5. Lama, M.P. "Internal displacement in India: Causes, Protection and Dilemmas" in *Forced Migration Review*, August 2000. Global IDP Project, Switzerland.
6. Mehta, P. (1998), *A Psychological Strategy for Alternative Human Development- Indian Performance since Independence*. Sage Publications, New Delhi.
7. World Refugee Survey, Washington, 2000; Walter Fernandes, Director of the Programme of Tribal Studies of the Indian Social Institute; Hampton J. (ed.), *Internally Displaced People*; A *Global Survey*, Earthscan Publication Limited, London, 1998.

4

Sounds of Silence: A Sterile Promontory of Development and Displacement in the Narmada Valley

— *Dr. Prashant Negi**

Wheresoe'er the traveler turns his steps,
He sees the barren wilderness erased,
or disappearing.

William Wordsworth, Excursion, 1814

A Congregation of Vapours: Origin, and the History of the Narmada Valley Project

The construction of dams on the river Narmada [it is the fifth longest river of India, 1312 kms and as a result of the Narmada Valley project (hereafter NVP), it will start flowing north from the south Gujarat village Navagam instead of west, onto the Arabian ocean] in Central India and its impact on millions of people living in the river valley has become one of the most important social issues in contemporary India.[1]

The NVP is the single largest multipurpose river valley project in India and one of the largest in the world. The NVP in its entirety envisages the construction of thirty major dams of which ten will be on the river Narmada, and the rest on its tributaries which includes the construction of 135 medium and 3000 minor dams.

* *Type VI, Bunglow No-12, Richmond Estate, Jhaku Hill, Simla, H.P. –171001.*

The NVP aims to provide water to the drought prone districts of Saurashtra, Kutch, North Gujarat and some parts of Rajasthan. It will cost the exchequer about 5000 crores[2] (at 1988 base index), displace over 1 million people approximately[3], will submerge over 37,000 hectares of land, will cause a loss of standing forest cover worth 30,000 crores, and the environmental cost projected is estimated at a mind boggling 30,923 crores. Besides the rehabilitation aspect, there are apprehensions of double equity i.e. the cost of the project will be unevenly imposed on the poor and the benefits are unlikely to flow to them in a manner so as to overcome their initial social and economic disadvantage.[4]

Though opposition to the NVP has preoccupied us for the past twenty years, the antecedents of the projects can be traced back to nearly a hundred years. The First Famine Commission instituted by the British in 1901, first envisaged harnessing the waters of the river Narmada.[5] While the initial studies were conducted after 1946, the Provinces (the present day States of Gujarat, Maharashtra, Madhya Pradesh and Rajasthan) could not agree upon the principle issue of debate--the sharing of water of the river Narmada. Pandit Jawaharlal Nehru (the then Prime Minister of India) inaugurated the project in 1960 and thus the construction of the project was deemed to have begun. From the 1960s until 1978 the main actors in the political drama of NVP were the representatives of the different States deposing before the Narmada Water Disputes Tribunal (hereafter NWDT). The NWDT was set up in 1969 to resolve the dispute between the states; it submitted its report in 1978. Final planning, allocation of finances and actual work on the project commenced only after the submission of the report by the NWDT.[6]

The Sardar Sarovar Project (hereafter SSP) in Gujarat is the second largest dam of the NVP in term submerged and the population displaced, though its construction began in 1961, it only gathered speed after the World Bank decided to fund the project in 1985.[7] The SSP is intended to harness the waters of the Narmada for irrigation, drinking water and power generation. A 445-foot high dam is being built at Navagam in

Gujarat from where a network of canals will branch out to irrigate 1.8 million hectares of this drought prone State and supply drinking water to over 40 million people. However, these claims have been closely examined and appear to be implausible. The project appears to make hefty promises, and all it takes is a cursory look at the current availability of power and irrigation potential in the country and one is struck by the puniness of the promised benefits from the project (for further references see the Working Group Report on the Irrigation Sector).[8]

The damming of the Narmada will create a vast puddle, submerging approximately 37,000 hectares of land. In all, the Government estimates that about 152,000 people or 27,000 families will be directly affected by the displacement due to the dam.[9] The affected include not only the people in the submergence area but also those displaced by construction of the infrastructure and the canal, by compensatory afforestation, by secondary displacement and more. When these people are added to those living in the submergence area the number may as well swell up to a million. Incredibly enough, the compensation package is only applicable to those classified as 'project affected persons' or 'oustees' and since most of the people have not been classified accordingly, they are not entitled to any compensation. The compensation package for the people classified as 'project affected' varies from State to State and it appears to be highly unlikely that it will ever be delivered. Several recent studies have shown that resettlement has considerably worsened the lives of the few families that have shifted so far from the place of their habitation and that their is sufficient indication that satisfactory rehabilitation is virtually impossible for a number of reasons.[10]

Out of 245 villages to be submerged by the reservoir of the dam, 19 lie in Gujarat, 33 in Maharashtra and 193 in Madhya Pradesh. While the 37,000 in the villages of Gujarat and Maharashtra are almost all hill Adivasis (read tribals), the submergence area of Madhya Pradesh consists of two distinct zones. The uppermost reaches of the reservoir will flood land in the plains of Nimar, Part of Dhar and Khargone district of

Madhya Pradesh. Here, the Narmada flows through a fertile valley, settled by a mixed population dominated by the Hindus of the Patidar caste. Two-thirds of the displacement due to the dam will occur in Nimar. Roughly a third of the 100,000 people being displaced by the NVP are Adivasis (classified as Scheduled Tribes by the Constitution of India) and because they have been largely assimilated into the dominant Hindu caste structure they do not share the distinctive cultural identities of their cousins living in the hills. Downstream of Nimar, the river cuts through the Vindhya and Satpura mountains, forming the boundary between Maharashtra and Jhabua districts of Madhya Pradesh (of which Alirajpur is a part). The river here is bounded by steep hills, fissured by paths of tributaries into escarpments where, on the north bank, live the hill adivasis of Alirajpur. Approximately 15,500 of them, including the population of Anjanvara, will be affected by the submergence. From here the river flows through to the dam site in Gujarat and then to the sea.

Although the government, claims to be a State of distibutive justice in its democratic form, and legitimize its claims to the moral uniqueness of its development policies, and to the self-evidently superior form of politics, it then deviates from the rationality of it's purpose, functions and practical meaning[11], to drastically alter the lives the people it has not even bothered to consult or inform. In Anjanvara for instance, the first information about the dam came from the surveyors of Central Water Commission, who came to place the place the stone markers to indicate the reservoir levels.[12]

In fact all the development activities in the submergence zone have been suspended, as these areas are of uncertain future.

Despite the large number of people affected, despite the enormity of change in their lives, there is no government-sponsored system of information that respects the people's right to know. In 1986 for instance, an independent survey discoverd that, contrary to the claims of the goverment, no one in Alirajpur had been issued Land Acquistion notices.[13] Most of the villagers in Anjanvara were also not appraised of their right under the NWDT Award.

In 1998, the Chairman of Narmada Valley Development Authority (NVDA), Mr. S.C. Varma resigned amongst skepticism of the government resolve to rehabilitate the displaced population.

The project has been termed as being a 'Socially unjust, economically unviable and environmentally catastrophic and a symbol of destruction,[14] by the critics who question the 'unholy objective' of the project which 'sacrifices' people belonging to the lower strata of the society.[15] In view of the above and considering the fact that Narmada is not the last white elephant to be foisted on us, a comprehensive review of the project seems to be an understatement.

The social, economics and environmental costs of the Narmada Valley Project completely outweigh its benefits. Clearly the planning and implementation of the project does not include the participation of the affected population and is a callous violation to their rights to information, cultural autonomy and choice.[16]

If It be Not Now Yet It Will Come: The Nature of Development

'Legend has it that the Narmada, in a fit of anger turned her back on her suitor, the Son river, and became one of the country's few west flowing river's. If she could hear her misguided champions she could her anger again'.[17]

The biggest arguments against the big dams are their exorbitant costs, long gestation periods and poor productivity. Though, the government argues for the need to create potential, but is not the same as potential being utilized to its optimum; potential is supposed to be created once the reservoir and the distributive system are in place but unbelievingly no provision is made in the original estimates for leveling of land, field channels, control devices to be installed before the farmers can actually irrigate his lands. In fact, most of the ills of the big dams arise from this omission. The big dam sector is accentuated by an almost complete process of collapse since Independence, with a virtual scramble for big dams without adequate studies, finds and time frame. Besides, estimates are deliberately kept low; to achieve desired internal rates of returns, and to make the projects more acceptable to the public. Thus, a vicious circle of projects languishing for the lack of funds and revision of estimates sets into motion, with overruns becoming the order of the day. Further, the big dam sector also suffers from internal weakness, which are difficult to overcome. It is extremely wasteful of the very resources it professes to nurture, as there is a massive loss of water due to evaporation and seepage losses. The big dams are also vulnerable to premature siltation and thence the loss of storage capacity due to denudation and soil erosion in their watershed, besides contributing towards water logging and salinization of land (India allows 36% of its land to be damaged by salinization[18]), and exerts an incalculable human suffering by uprooting communities from their original habitats.

To say, power helps in production, is for the general good, and is a *'sine qua non'* for progress does not camouflage the fact that electricity is not the resource as it is made out to be today. Though, planners allocate 1/5th of the total resources to the power sector alone, its record is but abysmal, considering the fact that the only energy accounted for is commercial and the rest is consumed free as it is collected free as fuel wood and at a great expense of human labor (the distance an average woman walks per year to find fuel wood- 1400 kms).[19] If then, one looks at the needs of the neediest, it is futile pointing to electricity (it is believed that only 14% of the Indian villages can afford electricity), as a resource for progress.[20]

"On the one hand, it is seen as a war between modern, rational, progressive forces of 'Development' *versus* a sort of neo-Luddite impulse – an irrational, emotional 'Anti-Development' resistance, fuelled by an Arcadian, pre-industrial dream. On the other, as a Nehru vs. Gandhi contest".[21] The debate is not just the 'big *versus* small' slanging but the entire developmental procedure is being questioned. If the policies followed in the last twenty years of encouraging capital and resources intensive inputs in agriculture are to continue together with a highly selective pattern of industrialization (mirrored in uneven urbanization) there is no way of reducing the nations dependence on such projects. Therefore, it necessary to evolve and mobilize a panoply of strategies, which span the not only the ideological spectrum of development but which also include within it, the colors of environmentalism, decentralization, sustanability, participation, anthropomorphic sensitiveness, ecology etc.

From an abstract, idealized expectation towards the need to represent entails a wisdom for which the need is dire and the need is now.

State and Bureaucratic Rationalization: Aiming Low (The Official Stand)

Despite the terrible social, environmental and economic record of the large dams, large dam project continue to be proposed and built. The dam industry juggernaut maintains its momentum because constructing dams benefits powerful political and economic interests, and because the planning, promoting and building dams is usually secretive and insulated from democratic dissent (such an perception has led to certain ideological questions which challenge the very tenets of development i.e. development for whom? and who pays for whom?). Similarly, taking the same plane of the argument the official sources believe that the rehabilitation norms adopted by the Gujarat government in the instance of the NVP are the most liberal in the country.[22]

Those who suffer from these projects are rarely able to hold the dam building bureaucracies accountable for their actions. A majority of large dam projects have been built by the State agencies and their poor economics performance has invariably been obscured behind a veil of public subsidies.[23]

The gargantuan scale of large dams, and their seeming ability to bring powerful and capricious natural forces under their control, gives them a unique hold on the human imagination. Perhaps more than any other technology, massive dams symbolize the progress of humanity from a life ruled by nature and superstition vanquished by rationality. They also symbolize the might of the State that built them, making large dams a favourite of nation-builders and technocrats.

When a dam is given such a powerful symbolic role, its economic and technical rationale and potential negative impacts fade into insignificance in the decision-making process.

There are a number of recurrent ideological themes in the writings and speeches of the proponents of large dams. One is the 'taming' of the 'wild' or 'turbulent' rivers, the appeal of which seems to be rooted in the biblical exhortation to go forth and subdue nature; another is the comparison of dams to temple and other places of worship. Probably the most common refrain is that undammed rivers are 'wasted'. Politicians and technocrats have for most of this century expounded that a river has no value unless it is in some ways controlled (and not just used) by human. This belief negates the intrinsic worth of rivers—the veins of hydrological cycle, shapers of the landscapes, and providers of life to many of the earth's species– it negates their cultural, aesthetic and spiritual importance, and it negates the economic value of unregulated rivers to the hundreds of millions of people who depend on them for drinking water, food, transport and other uses. The 'wasted river' ideologues are justifying not the human use of rivers, but the expropriation of rivers from one set of users to another.

The NVP was probably guided by political expediency, as it sidelined its own guidelines before commissioning the project. In the Seventh Five Year Plan, it was categorically stated that one of the major objectives of the Plan was to restrict new starts to medium and heavy irrigation projects in drought prone, tribal and backward areas with an emphasis on minor projects, which will get completed quickly and reap benefits immediately.[24] Development it seems is subservient to short-term political gains. Rajni Kothari, believes that the government's tactics arise out of neo-fascist tendencies, which seek to stifle all dissent and usher in an authoritarian State.

Though the Planning Commission Report, in 1980, stated that returns from irrigated land, in term of yield and finance are disappointing and that macro level projects seldom serve the interests of those with micro level incomes,[25] it accorded the project an investment clearance in October 1988, with certain preconditions:

The State government's to give priority to the NVP/SSP in the Eighth Plan, so that adequate funding matches the construction schedule, to complete ground water and drainage balance studies, the government's to submit a detailed report on such studies to the Planning Commission with achievements duly vetted by the Central Water Commission, and the government's to set up water rates suitably to ensure that annual revenue is accrued etc.

The Planning Commission also give statistical data to support its clearance of the project, the total irrigation potential to be created would be 1.79 million hectares and would benefit 12 out of 19 drought prone districts, the agricultural production was targeted to go up by 45% as a result of improved irrigation, the drinking and power problems of nearly 131 cities and 4720 villages will be addressed by the project and there will be generation of 49.44 lakh man years of direct and 42.71 years of indirect employment.[26]

The SSP is seen to be the only 'escapes route' by the political leadership of the Gujarat, as the project has assumed such sentimental dimensions that none dares to speak against it. It binds all the segments of the society and no political party can survive in Gujarat if its commitment to the project is suspicious, in fact the people in the State view the project as the next best thing after Sardar Patel.[27] The political leadership's thinking is in line with the argument that injection of fresh water into Gujarat will improve the state of environment.

The government of Gujarat has by far been the worst critic of the environmental lobby and the most vociferous supporter of the project. The opposition to the project has evoked extreme negative reactions from the government with the Narmada controversy turning into a political football and the debate being reduced to a name calling exercise by the government regularly labeling the critics of the project as 'canards', 'air conditioned critics'[28], 'vested interests', being 'outside agent'[29] and being a part of the 'imperialist controversy' and advocates of 'anti-development' and 'urban based lobbies'. The Gujarat government even went to the extent of calling the alliance between the Narmada Bachao Andolan (hereafter NBA), and the 'newly formed bandwagon of environmentalism' in the West as 'sheer opportunism'.[30] They rejected foreign intervention in the internal affairs of the country and for proliferating consumption, which has set wrong standards in the world and has done irreparable damage to the Earth. Herein, the dichotomy is acutely visible with the government first recognizing that environmental damage has been inflicted but at the same time demarcating the damage by asking for non-interference. The claims of the critics have been time and again dismissed by the government, one such instance is that of the assumed water flow of the project, which was found to be 28 million acre feet and was to be allocated to Gujarat and Madhya Pradesh at the ratio of 1 for 2, the critics claiming that 23 millions acre feet will be available have been dismissed by Khosla Committee, NWDT and the Sardar Sarovar Narmada Nigam, the Nigam itself had been cumulatively monitoring the water flow between 1986-1989 and had found it be 28 million acre feet[31], in another instance, Mr. P.A. Raj (Vice-Chairman & Managing Director) contested the claims of losses due to forest submergence. According to him the total losses due to submergence of forests were Rs. 31,406 crores (Rs. 25,306 crores in Narmada Sagar project and Rs. 6,100 crores in Sardar Sarovar) and not Rs. 40,000 crores (Rs. 33,000 crores in Narmada Sagar project and Rs. 7,000 cores in Sardar Sarovar) as projected by the critics.[32] He was also quoted to cite the total benefits of the project being in the tune of Rs. 68, 750 crores.

In September 1988, Mr. S. Mehta (Chairman of the Sardar Sarovar Narmada Nigam and Former Finance Minister of Gujarat) labeled the environmental argument as an 'uneducated broadside'. He divided the critics into three categories: Those concerned with rehabilitation, those opposed to big dams and abstract environmentalists.[33]

The environmental objections of the activists towards the project are more often than not contested by the government.

While defending the claim of reservoir induced seismicity, the Sardar Sarovar Narmada Nigam says that only 4 out of 500 big dams in the world have experienced reservoir induced seismicity and that the project has been designed by experts from Earthquake Engineering School of Rourkee and CWPRS of Pune, with advice from World Bank consultants Dr. Clugh and Dr. Blot of Berkeley University.[34] The then Union Minister for State for Water Resources, Mr. Manubhai Katadia was quoted as saying "studies take time and the country cannot maintain status quo on environmental issues".[35] There seems to be little rationale and pragmatism in the speech of the minister, it seems that apart from the government everyone realizes the mutual exclusiveness between the eco-system and any development activity that intrudes upon it. The government of Gujarat sees the dam as *'fait accompli'* and as 'life line' of the State and always remain anxious to ensure that nothing impedes the progress of the project. For instance, the Chief Minister of Gujarat, Mr. Amarsinh was known to assert both publicly and privately that he would resort to 'any means' necessary to counter resistance to the project.[36]

The government of Gujarat went to the extent of invoking the Officials Secrets Act of 1923, on January 30th 1989, when lawyers and other activists assembled in Kevadia colony near Bharuch, where official of the dam site were housed. Twelve villages around the project were declared as prohibited and anyone entering them without permission was liable to be arrested. The police presence was stepped up in the area and they were know to interrogate people day and night. Activities of protest and restlessness were quelled by the contractors in connivance with the police to the extent that locals always viewed accidents resulting in death as State managed.[37]

Such measure were viewed as an abuse of the draconian law that the British had incorporated into a statute six decades ago and as an antithesis to a democratic and an open society.

Infringement to the right of protest has often given way to a suspicion that the government are enormous as the project affected persons and their representatives desirous of acquiring information about the project can be jailed for up to

14 years. The law enforces çan frustrate, inhibit and threaten the attempts to make a case against the project by suppressing the right to information.

There are many even in the highest echelons of the Central Government and the World Bank who have grave misgivings about the project. Dr. Swaminathan (architect of the Green Revolution in India), was for incorporating environmental principles into every sector of the Eighth Five-Year Plan. From the beginning the World Bank has been playing an ambiguous role in its commitment to the project. On one side it exercised caution in funding the project as it believed that large dams have unforeseen consequences, demanding environmental appraisals of the project and on the other reaffirmed its commitment to the project.[38]

On 20th August 1989, Prime Minister Rajiv Gandhi while addressing irrigation minister conference expressed his dissatisfaction over surface irrigation projects due to their high costs, long gestation periods and poor productivity.[39]

"Big projects provide no irrigation, no water, no increase in production and no help in the daily lives of the people".[40]

What seems to be very conveniently forgotten is the fact that economic and developmental benefits should be viewed and evaluated against the totality of their nature and human costs and that developmental democracy and environmental sanity both require the synthesis of this rationale. If nothing else it demolishes the myth that environment is a non-political issue. Apparently it is entirely political for the simple reason that it concern that use of natural resources to which competing classes and communities lay claim and also because it entails the question of power , who yields it? And who exercises it? Specifically in relation to mega-projects the line of divide is between people who stand to gain and people who stand to be displaced. The question at the core of the issue is; Who benefits? Who pays the cost in social terms?[41]

People's Agencies: Pulling Out All the Stops

The first stirring of protests against the SSP started in 1978 in Nimar immediately after the Narmada Water Dispute

Tribunal gave its award. Arjun Singh, a leading politician from Congress (I), mobilized people in Nimar around the issue of displacement under the banner of Nimar Bachao Andolan. It is said that even though the movement worked well within the structures of party politics, participation at rallies was much larger than anything seen today. However, after winning the State elections on the platform that pledged support for the movement, Arjun Singh promptly ditched it.

After that the movement was directionless and collapsed.

The second attempt to organize the movement started when Medha Patkar, a social scientist from TISS (Tata Institute of Social Sciences), Bombay, started working in the SSP submergence zone villages in Maharashtra. In 1987, Patkar came to Nimar to build opposition to the SSP and thus started an epic resistance to the project. The NVP is a massive scheme and was resisted as whole but it has to be understood that was difficult of locally oppose all dams. Therefore the NBA concentrated its efforts on collective action against two of the largest dams of the NVP—the SSP and the Narmada Sagar Dam. Initially the NBA did not challenge the overall validity of the SSP but only concentrated on the issue for organising people for adequate rehabilitation. However, when it became apparent that it was virtually impossible for the State to properly rehabilitate the 'project affected people', and moreover, that the project was questionable on other grounds as well, it demanded total rejection of the project and voiced it in the slogan, *Koi nahin hatega! Baandh nahin benega!* (No one will move! The dam will not be built!).

The NGO's espousing the cause of the oustees in the Valley split into two major groups in August 1988. Groups such as ARCH-Vahini continued to concentrate on the objective of improved settlement and by contrast the NBA took an anti-dam stand.

Popular mobilization against the SSP has been augmented by co-operation from three broad based categories of NGO's and mass movements. The environmentalists and civil liberty groups, the rural organizations (Narmada Ghati Navnirman

Samiti, Narmada Dharagrast Samiti, Narmada Asargrast Sangarsh Samiti, Lok Adhikar Sangh etc) and the international organizations. In 1989, three US based NGO's – the Environmental Defence Fund, Environmental Policy Institute and the National Wildlife Federation, urged the United States Congress to compel the World Bank to withdraw from SSP. Their lobbying resulted in some of the most unprecedented ever taken by the World Bank , it first agreed to appoint an independent team to review the environmental and displacement impact of the dam[42] and then due to mounting pressure from international NGO's withdraw from the project in March, 1993, in a move that was preempted by the Government of India's refusal to accept the final allocation of funds for the project (incidentally both these events are of significant importance, as it was for first time that World Bank had independently reviewed a project that it had funded and then had subsequently withdrawn from it). Similarly, the persistent efforts of the Friends of Earth in Japan convinced the Japanese Government to suspend its aid to the SSP.

In March 1990, Baba Amte left his Ashram in Anandwan (Maharashtra), to live and join the protest in the Narmada Valley with a resolve that he will "submerge in the submergence of that sarovar" and that "till my nostrils breath, nobody is going to fill dams at Sardar Sarovar and Narmada Sagar". His new ashram in the valley provides testimony for hope in life, he has planted Banyan saplings (slow growing tree that take years to reach their majestic size)– an assertion of the belief that the valley will not drown.

These diverse tactics, aimed at several different audiences, have been employed as a part of a coordinated strategy to fight the dam at all levels—the international financial institutions, the national and State governments, and that mysterious but powerful force—public opinion.

The gathering forces of opposition against the SSP have their center in the valley, mainly in Madhya Pradesh and Maharashtra, among the people threatened with displacement. Since 1988, the inhabitants of the submergence area have been demonstrating their determined refusal to move from their land. Since then the years have been marked by continuous protest; survey work on the project has been disrupted, submergence markers placed by the surveyors have been removed and sent to State capital, official of the project including those of the World Bank teams have been mobbed and sent back, project authority offices have been forced to close down, the bridges and guest houses has been delayed.[43]

People have held demonstrations, launched relay hunger strikes, and even though the dam is being built and the scheduled submergence looms near, people have, by and large, not moved from their homes.

The constant passive resistance to the project has been punctuated by larger demonstrations, exhibited by the Andolan's strength in the valley.

The Andolan has also initiated litigation in the State courts challenging improper land acquisition and forcible evictions, State repression and denial of constitutionally guaranteed right to life. It also initiated litigation in the highest court of the land, the Supreme Court. The case was filed in 1994 on the basis that the costs of the dam would overrun its benefits, that the basic environmental studies were either not initiated or that they were bypassed and that there was no land available for rehabilitation. The initiation of litigation also meant that till the matter was subjudice construction at the dam site would deem to have stopped. The judgement pronounced was a mix-bag for both the NBA and the 'project affected persons'. The Supreme Court of India disposed off NBA's public interest litigation against SSP in its majority judgement of Chief Justice Anand and Justice Kirpal and on 18th, October 2000, allowed the work on the dam to resume for immediate construction. The judgement cleared the construction of the SSP dam upto 90 meters. Experts believe that this was an analysis of averred facts placed before the Supreme Court by the Government of Madhya Pradesh. For the first time the Supreme Court applied the 'Principle of Lashes' (the principle refers to a case being time barred if not up for hearing within a stipulated period of time) while deciding a public interest petition, prior to this judgement the principle was usually applied to individuals. It was only the minority judgment of Justice Baraucha who ruled that all the three conditions were flouted by the NVDA, which came as a reprieve to the efforts of the NBA.

The events this year may be a watershed for the Andolan and the fate of the project.

The arguments of NBA have received commendable support, time and again from independent and government research organizations.

Among them were:

(i) Planning Commission Report (1980) concludes that returns from irrigated land in terms of yield and finance are disappointing.[44]

(ii) NGRI (National Geophysical Research Institute) reported that Narmada Valley lies in a seismic zone prone to earthquakes.[45]

(iii) According to the document submitted by the Narmada Valley Development Authority to the Ministry of Environment (MoE) the environmental cost of the project would be a mind boggling Rs. 30,923 crores, incidentally the dam itself in 1988, was estimated at Rs. 25,000 cores. The document confirms the fears of the environmentalists, contradicted the claims made by the government and called out to categorically defer the project till 1989, by which time the data from various studies would be made available to access further environmental damage, thereby implying that the figure of Rs. 30,923 crores itself was an approximation on the lower side.[46]

(iv) In April 1989, an appraisal team sent by the World Bank expressed dissatisfaction with Relief and Rehabilitation work.[47]

(v) Lokayan, a Delhi based NGO, concluded in its report that neither the Central Government nor the three States had fulfilled the three conditions suggested by the World Bank. The three conditions were:

(a) The Governments of Madhya Pradesh and Maharashtra should promulgate official policies on

Relief and Rehabilitation in compliance with the NWDT and the agreement between the Central Government and the World Bank.

(b) Forestland controlled by the Center must be released in all the three States (unless in a special case the Center cannot do so).

(c) Crucial environmental studies be initiated at the earliest. They should include the following aspects: seismicity, public health, treatment to the catchment area, the carrying capacity and the compensatory afforestation.[48]

(vi) BNHS (Bombay Natural History Society) has suggested the scrapping of the project.[49]

(vii) The Environmental Defense Fund, based in the United States and Multiple Action Research Group (MARG), New Delhi, saw the investment of Non-Resident Indians into the project as a 'wasted treasure' and said that the NRI's were being 'stonewalled' by the Gujarat government by overplaying the role of the World Bank in the project.[50]

(viii) A study conducted by Vijay Pranjpye, sponsored by the Indian National Trust for Art and Culture (INTACH), concluded that the project is not viable even under the Central and State governments to an intolerable level of public and foreign debt.[51]

(ix) A study conducted by the *Tata Institute of Social Sciences*, reported a high mortality (44 deaths between May, 1985 and August 1989) rate among those settled in Parveta in the Narmada Valley. For the first time the reports of human right abuse by the State came into the foreground.[52]

(x) Vijay Pranjpye of ECONET, Pune calculated the cost benefit ratio of the dam to be 1:17:1, which fell short of Planning Commissions, stipulated ratio of 1:5:1. Earlier the TECS (Tata Economic Consultancy Service) has calculated the ratio to be 1:39:1, leaving out several related constructions. The government of Gujarat calculated the ratio to be less than 1:1 (C.C. Patel, July

1988). This negative ratio meant that the project was economically unviable and therefore it was decided that the original schedule of the project of 17-22 years should be reallocated to 10 years, again Patel was quoted to cite the cost benefit ratio as being 1:12:1. According to experts such quantification was done on the basis of data provided by the government.[53] How the Planning Commission cleared the project, which at no stage fulfilled its stipulated requirements, remain a mystery?

(xi) Sandra Postel, Vice-President of Worldwatch, a Washington based environmental group contended that the project was extravagant and suggested a departure to small and environmentally protective schemes such as moderate reservoirs, check dams, micro catchments and percolation tanks and added that such measures would reduce the cost spent her hectare by half.[54]

(xii) In the Indian Agricultural Economy Conference, Prof. H.M. Dasarda, brought attention to the under utilization of the created water potential and a very, very poor quality of the irrigation water provided.[55]

(xiii) West German Minister for Economic Affairs, Mr. Hans Peter Repnik visited Narmada Valley and expressed his reservations of the project.[56]

(xiv) In a study conducted for the World Commission on Dams (WCD) by India Country Study (ICS), a consultant team of five experts concluded that the M&M (major, medium and minor) irrigation projects are unviable "given their high capital costs, long gestation periods, the environmental and social costs, it contended that hydropower development was not the preferred option for power generation when compared to other sources".[57]

A Little Patch of Ground, Living on the Margin: Social Objections

The debate about the social impacts of dams resolves primarily around whether the positive economic benefits of dams outweigh the costs, the way in which positive and negative impacts are distributed among people, and whether such a distribution is equitable.[58] There has been particular concern about impacts on indigenous people, women and reservoir evacuees. Issue of equity, concern the normative issue of fairness or justice of the existing or planned distribution of impacts.

The assessment of social impacts is problematic. First, social impacts can be both positive (new access to irrigation water) and negative (resettlement etc). Second, social impacts can be direct or the result of a cascade, where environmental impacts generate economic impacts, and these in turns cause social impacts. Third, social and environmental or economic impacts from which they stem can be interlocked in complex and profound ways. Positive and negative impacts can both flow from the same environmental change. Fourth, the positive and negative impacts of large dams are not evenly spread and there can be significant disparities in impacts, particularly between less and wealthy groups and individuals; livelihoods are central to social impacts. Fifth, gender has been a missing element in impact assessment of large dams. Gender is one of the basic relational dynamics through which a community organizes itself. Dams affect men and women in different ways. An analysis of the social impacts of a dam that marginalizes gender can produce misleading conclusions, at variance with realities of both women and men, and the specific ways in which large dam affects them.

There a number of different ways to refer to those impacted by developmental projects. The debate on equity revolves around three main axes, which also reflects the divergence of view and perspectives. The first axis is based on a general balance sheet approach where the basic question is whether positive impacts of dam outweigh negative impacts. Proponents of dams tend to hold the view that if all the social and economic implications of most projects are taken into consideration, with clear description of all benefits that accrue to regions and nations as a whole, the advantages of these projects outweigh the disadvantages. For opponents of large dams, if all the social and environmental costs were taken into account, particularly how land and livelihood have been affected, the magnitude of the disadvantages of such projects would appear clearly and would call such interventions into question

The second axis concerns the extent to which those who bear the costs reap the benefits, or have access to the wealth generated by the project and vice versa. Those who receive more than they loose, would be gainers, and others would be losers. Opponents of large dams claim that displaced populations and riverine communities (losing their traditional sources of livelihood and exposed to water borne diseases) tends to be net losers as they are generally denied access to the benefits generated. Proponent's points to trickle down effects of dam and the fact that they ultimately benefit society at large, including locally affected groups.

The third axis compares the way the cost (taken separately) or benefits (consideration in isolation) of the project are distributed between selected groups, spatially (upstream or downstream, or among riparian States) or temporary (current and future generations) units or administrative entities. The most serious negative impacts of dams are due to the trauma of resettlement, or the socio-economic and cultural costs to displaced people who are not settled.

The displacement and rehabilitation of the people in Narmada Valley are, first and foremost, political issues[59], though they have also been seen as one of the most important social consequences of the project. Though official estimates of the exact number of people being displaced are unavailable, it is widely believed that approximately 1 million people will be displaced by the project. Added to this is the fact that Go I does not have an explicit national policy on settlement and rehabilitation.[60]

Though resettlement is the responsibility of relevant project authorities, it is widely believed that what the displaced get depends upon their political power and organizational skills. And given to this is the fact that if displaced people belong to the disadvantageous section there have been few instances of successful rehabilitation in India.

Until now the official was guided by the Land Acquisition Act of 1894, which provided for cash compensation for the displaced. An amendment introduced in 1984 allowed the State to provide for land as alternative compensation, but the provision of land is not legally binding on the State, it merely facilitates it. Both these Acts have totally ignored the rights of the landless, those customarily cultivating land and those who have locally recognized user right to land for compensation.

There is some controversy as to what would constitute an adequate resettlement package. Cash compensation alone, is a highly problematic formula. Several studies have shown , for instance, that if displaced persons are not used to handling large sums of cash compensation money can run through their fingers 'like water in a sieve'.[61] Moreover, cash compensation is usually much below the replacement value of land and if compensation level is adequate in principle, suitable land may be hard to find. Since switching to other bases of livelihood is of the quite difficult, cash compensation tends to end up being used as a temporary means of subsistence. The income criterion, however, does not take into account the role of environmental and common-property resources in the pre-displacement economy, nor does it give adequate recognition to other aspects of the quality of life that are threatened by the displacement process, such as family ties and community participation. The best way of guaranteeing sustainable livelihood, then, is the direct provision of land as compensation— the land for land policy. A land for land policy reduces the dislocation involved but land at the same time is highly contested resources in India and the land available is not only inferior, unproductive but it also available in limited quantities. The main alternative thence is employment-based compensation but here again there are frequent problems of inadequate employment opportunities as the number of displaced persons is generally larger than the opportunities that can be created for them. This is particularly the case when displaced persons have low levels of education and human resources. Even when employment criterion is feasible on an adequate scale, the transition out of a land-based economy can be quite problematic, if it disrupts important social and cultural roots of the displaced community. Resettlement policies, where they exist, sometimes allows for a flexible use of different bases of compensation and concentrate on the objective rather than the means to be used.

The World Bank for instance holds the view that the basic objective of the resettlement policy should be to ensure that the income of the displaced persons does not decline.[62]

One general flaw of most current approaches to resettlement policy is that the content of resettlement packages is left to government or project authorities. An entirely different approach would consist of leaving it to the displaced people to decide for themselves, what constitutes an adequate resettlement. This is one aspect of the ideas of voluntary resettlement and participatory development.

The Resettlement Policy in the Narmada Valley was guided by the NWDT, which gave its award in 1978, and adjudicated for sharing of water, by the riparian States. According to the award Rs. 600 crores were to be spent on rehabilitation (out of which Rs. 500 crores were to be spent on the oustees from Madhya Pradesh and Maharashtra who want to settle in Gujarat)[63], agricultural land equal to the land acquired or minimum of 2 hectares to be given to each family displaced, every son of the landed oustees who has reached the age of 21, to be treated as a family and entitled to 2 hectares of land (this clause also applied to joint holders of land, landless laborers and their major sons), residential plots of 500 square meters to be given to all oustees and their major sons, resettlement grant and grant-in-aid was payable, the Narmada Valley Development Authority was to liberalize subsidy norms and grant subsidy at the rate of 100% limited to Rs. 5000 crores, electricity and insurance cover was also to be given to all the displaced families. The NWDT stipulated that the 'standard of living' of displaced persons should not decline after resettlement. Though this principle is more acceptable than the other criterion, it leaves open the question so as to how the 'standard of living' is to be interpreted and assessed.

A broader definition, which takes into account all relevant aspects of the quality of life, is clearly needed, but little progress has been made in making such a definition operational.[64]

Displacement of people from their homelands and their eventual influx to urban areas often results in cultural alienation of the displaced people from their cultures. Coupled with it is the belief that the project is seen to be helping a handful of urban and rural elite to prosper, leading to further polarization of the society.

In February 1988, Chairman of the Narmada Valley Development Authority, Mr. S.C. Varma resigned to lead an agitation to safeguard the interest of the people being displaced. He seemed to be skeptical of the Gujarat and Madhya Pradesh government's promises that displaced people will be adequately compensated and rehabilitated. He admitted in his official capacity that the tribals, who have no legal rights over land will be thrown on roads and that all the cultivable land in Madhya Pradesh was authorisedly or unauthorisedly under the plough, that there was a little possibility of getting sizable blocks for allotment and that the cash compensation being offered was meagre and plagued by corruption.

Compensation for land in the NVP varied from Rs. 200-2000 to Rs. 40,000 per hectare for the politically connected.[65] In such condition the role of the 'dhantantra' (money power)[66] and the misuse of the official machinery in the distributive process have been the focus of sharply contested debates.

In September 1988, Mrinalini Sarabhai (Chairperson of Gujarat Handicrafts and Handloom Corporation) and a host of other eminent people like Dr. M.S. Swaminathan, Dr. Satish Dhawn, Justice V.R. Krishna Iyer signed a memorandum addressed to Prime Minister Rajiv Gandhi highlighting the enormous social, cultural, economic and environmental cost of the Narmada project.[67] In October 1988, the Department of Environment, GoI, expressed unequivocally its reservations regarding the rehabilitation of 1.71 lakh people (this incidentally were the official figures quoted for the people being displaced). Noting that 40,000 hectares of land required for rehabilitation was not even identified, let alone surveyed for water availability or for the magnitude of reclamation work.

The minutes of the Narmada Control Authority (NCA) meeting in November 1988 recorded the fact that all of the 65,000 hectares of land identified for rehabilitation in Madhya Pradesh and Maharashtra was saline. In 1989 the Status Report of Narmada Control Authority reported that:

'Progress in planning rehabilitation is neither satisfactory nor adequate.'[68]

According to Mr. S.S. Varma, Union Welfare Secretary and Mr. Geetakrishnan, Union Secretary of Environment, land for resettlement was not available and there was no possibility of denotifying denuded forestland. Hence it becomes apparent that private purchase of land would be required but this would pose further problems, as the oustees will be reallocated in small pockets leading to dislocation of the tribal culture and intermixing of the tribal and non-tribals communities.[69]

Dr. A.S. Desai, Director of Tata Institute of Social Sciences also urged the World Bank to take a closer look at the project keeping in mind the mechanics and methodology of the project and also the expenditure and purpose of the project. He called the project a proverbial case of development with deprivation as there exists a considerable distance between construction activity and rehabilitation work.[70] A Report of World Commission of Environment and Development titled 'Food 2000' noted the fact that socio-economic understand social disruption stemming from the displaced rarely get fair compensation for their losses.

In term of social impacts of dams, the World Commission on Dams (WCD) report mentions that the negative effects of the dams were frequently neither adequately assessed nor accounted for.[71] The range of these impacts is substantial, including on the lives, livelihood and the health of the affected communities dependent on the riverine environment:

(i) Some 40-80 million people have been physically displaced by dams worldwide.

(ii) Millions of people living downstream from dams– particularly those reliant on natural floodplain and fisheries— have also suffered serious harm to their livelihoods and the future productivity of their resources has been put to risk.

(iii) Many of the displacement were not recognized (or enumerated) as such, and therefore were not resettled or compensated.

(iv) Where compensation was provided it was often inadequate, and where the physically displaced were enumerated, many were not involved in resettlement programs.

(v) Those who were resettled rarely had their livelihoods restored, as resettlement programs have focused on physical reallocation rather than economic and social development of the displaced.

(vi) The larger the magnitude of displacement, the less likely it is that even the livelihoods of the affected communities can be restored.

(vii) Even in the 1990s, impact on downstream livelihoods were, in many cases, not adequately assessed or addressed in the planning and design of large dams.

In sum, the report demonstrated a generalized lack of commitment, or lack of capacity to cope with displacement. In addition, large dams have also had significant adverse effects on cultural heritage through the loss of cultural resources of the local communities and the submergence and degradation of plant and animal remains, burial sites and archeological monuments.

In light of the inequities existing in the distribution of the costs and benefits in terms of displacement and rehabilitation, the NVP seems to unacceptable on equity grounds. In any event, the true economics profitability of the NVP remains elusive as the environmental and social costs of the project were poorly accounted for in economic terms. More to the point, failures to account adequately for these impacts and to fulfil commitments that were made have led to the impoverishment and suffering of millions, giving rise to growing opposition to the dam by affected communities. Innovative examples of processes for making reparations and sharing project benefits are emerging that provide hope that past injustices can be remedied and future ones avoided.

Therefore, it is only desirous that the formulation of a rehabilitation policy be comprehensive and that in order for it to retain the 'welfare and total' perspectives it should get rid of its inherent assumptions of displacement being inevitable by delimiting itself from economic resettlement emphasizing on the 'balance-sheet approach' and by understanding that the very nature of national development has to change.

Alternatives to a Process of Knowledge: That We Would Do, We Should Do When We Would: A Methodological Question

The need of the hour is to stitch a more stronger, resilient and colorful people centric; people sensitive tapestry sculpted by the process of shared understanding. We must ensure that development is sustainable and more humane. To explain how to develop water in ways that do not exhaust either our constituents of the resources we all depend on, we must go beyond platitudes. Our healing must emerge not through anecdotes, but through a complex, coherent and cohesive argument that shows clearly where we have been, what happened, why we are in conflict, and how we can, with proper understanding heal ourselves.

Therefore, the theory of development should generate, accumulate and transfer knowledge and know-how on human aspects of economic, political, cultural and social change, deal with the challenges of transformation and change within the already expanding horizon of availability of development options and the emergence of the contemporary environmental crises as global phenomenon.

That involves first shedding of misconceptions. Today's demands are too complex, our technology too advanced, our constituency too diverse, our options too numerous to allow just one solution. One way is to incorporate interdisciplinary, comparative and pluralistic approach to the analysis of global and local issues in development and environment. Given such an orientation, much of the argument provided should be articulated in a multi-disciplinary setting: as problems are typically multifaceted, their analysis and solutions require inputs from a broad array of disciplines and perspectives, thereby enhancing the analytical capacities of the argument.

Moreover, the alternative theory of development, 'beyond development' etc. should advocate comparative analysis of societal problems, highlight similarities and commonalities as well as geographically, culturally and historically determined differences. By way of a process of critically attempts should be made to understand development and environment at local, national, regional and international levels in the wider contexts of the processes of globalization, dependency, modes of production etc. Though, the argument should be embedded in theory it must strive to embolden itself into the practice of development oriented capacities by providing an application-based research, to facilitate through comparative studies, processes by which societies could develop in sustainable and just ways and also to heighten awareness that acting in any historically or culturally specific context, be it spatially defined or within a network, requires insight into, as well as public control over, global processes of negotiation about, and the exchange of goods, services, capital, people and technologies.

The theory should provide an introduction to key substantial problems, concepts, theories and strategies in the reflection on and the practice of development. It should analyze development theories within (1) poverty, social exclusion and marginalization and (2) environmental degradation and resource conflict. Within these areas explicit attention must be given to the impact of structural adjustment, the role of the state, society, gender and the diversification of the rural livelihoods. The exploration of the interrelations between the individual and the collective and their broader historical and social context will enable the argument to locate itself within the wider political and economic processes.

The issues and the analytical responses to them must be treated in a historical perspective with due diligence being accorded to socio-economic, political, cultural dimensions and also to the intersectoral problems and approaches. The treatment in such a case should be both general and specific.

Within the large processes of social, economic and environmental transformation the focus should be on processes leading to social exclusion, environmental degradation, the public action undertaken by government or grass root organizations, analysis of development policies in the context of institutions, actors and political structures which are undergoing changes as a result of globalization and structural adjustment. The role of State and civil society organizations in policy formulation and implementation should also receive appropriate attention.

The theory should be organized around contrasting general paradigms (such as the neo-classical theory and its critics based approaches *versus* populism; rights approaches; and structure *versus* agency) as well a s around particular issues (for instance natural resource management, poverty, technology, rural conflicts and social movements and gender).

The theory of development should also borrows from the economics of development to be familiar with the development debates in the main areas of development economics, to be able to apply relevant areas of economic analysis to illuminate these debates and to be familiar with various schools of thought and be able to appreciate the importance of institutional factors, ownership and the role of socio-political forces within the context of the development debate. It should focus on two broad areas that are at the core of the development process and development policy debates. First, the determinant of economic growth, with emphasis on the conditions for sustainable human development. This should be introduced to understand the basic principles of traditional and new growth theories, the foundations of welfare economics and the relationship between long-run growth, on the one hand and human development and natural resource management, on the other. The second area of focus should be macroeconomics management and structural adjustment policies. Attention should be given to the role of the domestic and international finance in adjustment process. The objective here should be to integrate macroeconomic issue with macroeconomic processes.

Such an analytical, comprehensive, pluralistic and comparative alternative development theory is based on the assumption that alternatives development calls for constant innovation and is rooted in political, social, economic, cultural, and ecological dimensions and that crosscutting themes are synergies among social forces, governmental, the non-governmental sector, gender and ecological concerns and include the knowledge of general principles and main elements that are distinctively for alternative development. It involves familiarity with the differences between alternative development and mainstream development approaches, comparative experiences with alternative development, and relevant debates and criticisms of alternative development thinking and practice and the realization and incorporation of knowledge of the politics of development, international political economy and the politics of structural reform approaches and their alternatives. Given such an orientation the politics of development should be understood in the role that it plays in development processes and how power structure and political institution influence development outcomes and also in the current drive toward 'modernization revisionism' embedded in the triple discourse of democratization, human rights and good governance. The knowledge of politics of structural reforms is also important as it articulates the socio-economic and political impact of structural reforms on civil society, the State and the differential consequences of structural reforms, particularly on the excluded (minorities and women) and global projects (environment and social development).

The issue of sustainable development should also be discussed. Themes considered, as part of sustainable development such as green thinking and environment in international political relations and negotiations must be included.

The emphasis on women in the context of development and gender relations requires the analysis of women's agency from a historical, global and comparative perspective. The idea is to understand and conceptualize the feminist and the gendered analysis of the complex relationships between women's subordination and development. The emphasis is on (i) feminist theorizing on development – which includes a critique of modernity, modernization and development, (ii) Gender, economic restructuring and livelihood strategies providing an understanding of global processes of restructuring in urban and rural areas and (iii) Women organizing for change.

To confer legitimacy on such epochal decisions which involve people's lives, real development must be people-centred, while respecting the role of the State as mediating, and often representing, their interests. It is a time not to endorse globalization as led from above by a few men but to endorse globalization as led from below by all, an approach to global policy on development. In this approach, we must deal with the past before we can chart a course for the future. The integrity of our process determines the integrity of our product. Should we succeed the present age will be known as the Third Revolution, and it will not any more than the first two, be immediate.

REFERENCES

1. See www.narmada.org.
2. See *Indian Express*, Narmada Controversy, 3rd February 1988, New Delhi.
3. Roy Arundhati, The Greater Common Good, *Frontline* & also available in book form.
4. See *Patriot*, More on Narmada Water, 21st November 1989, New Delhi.
5. See *The Times of India*, Environmental cost of the Narmada plan high, 19th of July 1988, New Delhi.
6. *Kalpavariksh*, 1988, The Narmada Valley Project: A Critique, New Delhi.
7. In 1985 the World Bank enterd into a credit and loan agreement for $450 million, which at that time represented 18% of the cost of the dam and the power project 30% of the water delivery project. The World Bank had then estimated the cost of the project to be Rs. 13,640 crores. However cost escalation and devaluation of the rupee have made it difficult to estimate the total cost of the project. On the basis of figures included in Gujarat State budget, the total cost in 1992 terms should be around 20,470 crore rupees.
8. See *Hindustan Times*, Bajaj, J.K. Do we need Tehri?, 18th March 1990.
9. Morse. Bradford and Thomas Berger, Sardar Sarovar, *The Report of the Independent Review*, Resources Future International, Ottawa, 1992.
10. Bhatia. Bela, Forced evictions of the Tribal Oustees due to the Sardar

Sarovar project in Five Submerging Villages in Gujarat. Report submitted to the Gujarat High Court. Mimeo, 1993. See also, TISS (Tata Institute of Social Sciences). Sardar Sarovar Project: Review of Resettlement and Rehabilitation in Maharashtra, *Economic and Political Weekly* , Vol. 28: No. 34.

11. Apter, David. E, *Rethinking Development: Modernization, Dependency and Post-Modern Politics*, Sage Publications, 1987.
12. Bhaviskar. Amita, In *The Belly of The River: Tribal Conflicts over Development in the Narmada Valley*, Oxford, New Delhi, 1995.
13. MARG (Multiple Action Research Group), Sardar Sarovar Oustees in Madhya Pradesh: What do they know? (I) Alirajpur, New Delhi, 1986.
14. See *Hindu*, The P.M. urged to review Narmada Project, 24th January 1990. Madras.
15. See *The Times of* India, 7th June 1988, New Delhi.
16. Bhaviskar. Amita, *op. cit*.
17. See *Deccan Herald*, Don't damn Narmada, 30th September 1989.
18. See *Statesman*, Caution on irrigation, 20th January 1990.
19. See *Indian Express*, The case against big dams: First things first, 7th February 1990, New Delhi.
20. See *Times of India*, Dissent on big dams: First things first, 7th February 1990, New Delhi.
21. Roy Arundhati, *op. cit*.
22. See, *Hindustan Times*, Setback for Narmada Project cirtics. 6th August, 1989.
23. McCully Patrick, *Silenced Rivers: The Ecology and Politics of Large Dams*, Orient Longman Ltd., New Delhi, 1998.
24. See *Indian Express*, Continuing Opposition to Narmada Project, 18th October 1988, New Delhi.
25. See *Deccan Herald*, Large Dams, 22nd April, 1989.
26. See *Patriot*, Planning Commission clears Narmada Project, 6th October 1988, New Delhi.
27. See *Financial Express*, Disasters can be popular, 12th April 1989, New Delhi.
28. See *Patriot*, Opposition to Narmada decried, 20th September 1989, New Delhi.
29. See *Statesman*, The Unquiet Narmada, 17th October 1989, New Delhi.
30. See *Deccan Herald*, Don't damn Narmada, 30th September 1998.
31. See *Financial Express*, Fears over Sardar Sarovar allayed, 30th October 1989, New Delhi.
32. See *Patriot*, Narmada Sagar project. Gujarat going full steam ahead, 30th January 1990, New Delhi.
33. See *Indian Express*, Narmada Project Vital, September 26th 1988, New Delhi. Mr. Mehta conceived the project to be of vital importance to the State. It is supposed to provide 8 million acre feet of irrigation water, which will irrigate two-thirds of the draught prone areas and check the spread of crippling disease of flurosis. The soil in the distrcit of Saurashtra

is only nine inch deep and beneath it lies a rock containing fluoride, since both people and cattle depend on water from rock depths, they are prone to the disease.

34. See *Patriot*, Narmada Sarovar project: Gujarat going full steam ahead, 30th January, 1990, New Delhi.
35. See *Deccan Herald*, Safeguards impracticable: Ministers defend big power, irrigation projects, 1st February 1990.
36. See *Indian Express*, Under the Umbrella of Official Secrets Act, February 24th 1989, New Delhi.
37. *Ibid*.
38. See *Patriot*, World Bank firm on financing Sardar Sarovar, 8th November 1989, New Delhi.
39. See, *Financial Express*, A reservoir of problems, 21st August 1989, New Delhi.
40. See, *Indian Express*, The case against big dams, 7th February 1990, New Delhi.
41. See *Times of India*, Dissent on big dams; First things first, 7th Februray 1990, New Delhi.
42. In June 1992, The Independent Review submitted a highly detailed report, which was consistently and strongly critical of the project, as well as of the Bank for funding the SSP in violation of its own guidelines.
43. Bhaviskar. Amita, Op. Cit.
44. See *Deccan Herald*, Large dams, 22nd April 1989.
45. See *Indian Express*, Narmada controversy, 3rd February, 1989, New Delhi.
46. See Times of India, Environmental cost of the Narmada Plan high, 19th July 1988, New Delhi.
47. See *Statesman*, World Bank may stop funding, 30th June 1989, New Delhi.
48. *Ibid*.
49. See *Indian Express*, M.S. Varsity in a dilemma, 6th September 1989, New Delhi.
50. See *Hindustan Times*, NRI's being lured into the project, 19th May 1989, New Delhi.
51. See *Times of India*, Narmada project not viable: expert, 3rd September 1989, New Delhi.
52. See *Times of India*, NCA strictures resented, 12th January 1990, New Delhi.
53. See *Indian Express*, Continuing opposition to Narmada project, 18th October, 1988, New Delhi.
54. See *Statesman*, Caution on irrigation, 20th January 1990 New Delhi.
55. *Ibid*.
56. See *Indian Express*, Manekas's remark on Narmada, 6th February 1990, New delhi.
57. It also highlights the lack of legal framework, political will and planning infrastructure to mitigate and redress the substantial negative effects that large dams have on environment and society. The report also adds that the dams cater to the well to do, 62% of the population displaced is

that of tribals. Even the elctricity and irrigation benefits routinely by-pass the 'project affected persons' and are disproportionately consumed by the landed farmers and urban electricity consumers. Even the distribution of most of the costs and benefits of the large dams seem to accentuate socio-economic inequalities. It further states that the 'marginal contribution of large dams to increased food grains production (in India) is less than 19%", expose the poor track record of large dams in India on all accounts—social, economic, environmental, financial and notes that the 'cost are underestimated and benefits exaggerated so that the requisite B-C ratio is shown to have been arrived at'

For further reference see on the www.narmada.org. a press release by SANDRP (South Asian Network on Dams, Rivers and People), 20th September 2000.

58. Adams, William, *The Social impacts of large Dams: Equity and Distributional Issues,* Prepared for the World Commission on Dams, Final Version, November 2000.
59. Dreze Jean, Meera Samson, Satyajit Singh (eds), *The Dam and the Nation: Displacement and Resettlement in Narmada Valley,* Oxford University Press, New Delhi, 1997.
60. A draft National Policy has been prepared by the Ministry of Rural Development, but it is still at the stage of consideration by different ministries. A few state governments notably Maharashtra, Madhya Pradesh and Karnataka have framed their own policy.
61. Dhagamvar Vasudha, Rehabilitation: Policy and Institutional changes required, in Walter Fernandez & E.G. Thukrals (eds), *Development and Rehabilitation,* Indian Social Institute, New Delhi, 1989.
62. World Bank, *Resettlement and Rehabilitation in India,* 2 Volumes, India Department, World Bank, Washington DC, 1994.
63. See *Times of India,* Scheme for Narmada Project Oustees, 7th November 1988, New Delhi.
64. See Dreze Jean, Meera Samson and Satyajit Singh, *op. cit.*
65. See *Times of India,* Glimmer of hope in doomed town, 30th September 1989, New Delhi.
66. See *Times of India,* Suspend Narmada project, 24th January 1990, New Delhi.
67. See *Times of India,* Debate, Not witch hunt, 22nd September 1988, New Delhi.
68. See *Financial Express,* Narmada project oustees: Rehabilitation plan not satisfactory, 2nd May 1989, New Delhi.
69. See *Indian Express,* Land for oustees not available, 14th November 1988, New Delhi.
70. See *Times of India,* NCA strictures resented, 12th January1990, New Delhi.
71. *Dams and Development: A New Framework for Decision Making,* The Report of the World Commission on Dams, Earthscan Publications Limited, London and Sterling, November 2000.

5

Large Dams, Sustainable Development and Displacement

— *Dr. B. Eswar Rao Patnaik**

There has been a long standing debate among academicians, bureaucrats and irrigation experts on the pros and cons of major Irrigation Projects. Achievement of ecological balance in the economy has occupied the central place in the scheme of development in developing countries. The aim of the present paper is to analyse dispassionately the economics of major dams in the capital scarce and labour abundant economy of India. The scope of the present is limited to Narmada Multipurpose Project, Tehri Dam and Sardar Sarovar Project. Secondary data assembled from standard texts, reference journals and occasional newspapers provide materials for the current study. The study is organised into 4 sections.

Section-I, deals with introductory part of the study, various types of irrigation facilities available at country level.

Section-II carries us to a trip the credit side of dams. In Section-III, the debit side of dams is discussed. The policy prescriptions emerging from the study leading to conclusion are presented in Section-IV.

Section-I

Introduction

The one major issue in which the global society seems genuinely interested is environment . The situation is getting

* *Principal, S.B.R.G. Womer's College, Berhampur, Orissa.*

alarming day by day and the endeavour all over is how to overcome the burning problem. The factors fuelling the five are population explosion, deforestation, enormous demand on land for food and rapid industrialisation and urbanisation. The strains and stresses on the ecosystem raises the issue of compatibility of economic growth and environment. Acceleration of the pace of growth depends on the effectiveness of policy making in achieving the twin goals of development and ecological balance.

The perspective contained in the report of the World Commission on Dams released in London on November 16, 2000 are revealing. This first comprehensive, survey of dams presents a balance sheet of the benefits and adverse impact of these capital intensive infrastructure projects to. In balance, what emerges from the report is not a happy picture. The 45,000 large dams world wide have displaced 40 million to 50 million people, affected 60% of all rivers, have had an extensive negative impact on rivers and water shed and have failed to recover costs. Initial design of these must consider human and environmental costs, while estimating total costs.

India is a developing country, where 64% of population (1995) are dependent on agriculture and there is a wealth of substance in Nehru's belief that, dams are temples of modern India. India is one of the wettiest countries of the world, with an average rainfall of 1100 m.m. The planner's insistence on dams is plausible because, in India barring northern states, which get water from snow fed rivers also, all other parts of the country have to depend on monsoon rains for the supply of water. What is precarious is the availability of water for four months from mid-June to mid-October. Unless this supply is stored in artificially created reservoirs, it can not be available for use during the whole year. Till now, the economy is able to utilise only a quarter of rainfall it receives annually.

A perusal of plan priorities in India reveals that, the account of first six plans in India was on major and medium irrigation, which claimed a sum of rupees 72,000 crores at 96-97 prices (57.3% of outlay). The eighth five year went a step further in this direction and allocated Rs. 43,035 crores (76.3%

of outlay for major and medium irrigation works). The precedence accord by development planners of the country to major and medium irrigation projects over minor irrigation projects is evident, when we discern that, major and medium irrigation works have claimed the lion's share of resources i.e. 76.3% of total outlay in the ninth plan, as against the party share of 5.3% claimed by minor irrigation works.

One feather to the cap of plan exercises in India is the creation of the largest number of dams in the world i.e. 1580 major dams in 1985. These dams claimed a sum of Rs. 15,026 crores and cover nearly one per cent of total land area. In a way, the performance of major and medium irrigation project is in commensurate with the resources invested on them. The irrigation potential created by large and medium projects has gone up handsomely from 10 million hectares in 1950-51 to 33 million hectares in 1996-97. Thanks to irrigation sector, the wheels of agricultural progress were pushed forwards. Rudar Dutt reasons that, production of hydro-electric energy has risen smartly from 3 billion KWH in 1950-51 to 74.5 billion KWH in 1997-98. The gross area irrigated as a percent of sown area at country level works out to 38.2%, in 1997-98.

The neglect of tanks and minor irrigation works by policy makers is the eclipse on the rosy scene.

Table 1

Annual Water Resources of India and 2025

	Million Hectares Year 1974	2025
Total Precapitation	400	400
(a) Immediate evaporation.	70	70
(b) Run-off to surface water bodies.	115	115
(c) Percobation into the soil.	215	215
Water utilisation of which ground	38	105
Water contributes to	13	35
surface flows.	25	25

Source: Rudar Dutt and K. P. M. Sundaram *"Indian Economy"*.

Section – II

Development is a two-way process. It has not only to be induced from above. It should also emerge from below. People are directly affected from development and hence, they should be involved in planning as well as execution of development process. The critics of big dams can be grouped under two categories: (i) those environmentalists, who believe in maintaining classical, pre-industrial man- nature balance. (ii) Those activists who profess faith in small is beautiful and contend for many small dams and water-shed management instead of large dams. The second group of critics do not altogether oppose large dams but what they suggest is adoption of a humanitarian approach while executing mammoth irrigation projects.

Case Studies of Narmada Multipurpose Project Sardar Sarovar Project and Tehri Dam.

The Narmada Sagar multipurpose River valley project, which is believed to be the largest river project in India has a catchment area of 98,796 sq. kms. distributed over the three states of Madhya Pradesh, Maharashtra and Gujarat. The construction of 30 major, 135 medium and 3000 minor irrigation dams was contemplated by the project. The Sardar Sarovar Project, which is one of the rarest engineering feats, bestows multiple benefits on the people of Rajasthan, Maharashtra in general and Gujarat in particular. The I.B.R.D. has approved to sanction a loan amount of $300 million and I.D.A. has come upto finance credit worth R. $150 for Narmada canal and the distribution system.

The Tehri Dam Project which was implemented with Soviet aid was approved by Planning Commission in 1972. The dam will be the first highest – 260.5 mts. high dam in India, which will utilise the water of Ganges to generate 2400 M.W. peaking, irrigate 2.7 lakh hectares of land in Western U.P. and above all supply 300 cubic meters to Delhi.

The case for Narmada project arises from the topography of Western India, which is water scarce, receiving erratic monsoon spread over 30 days in a year. The economy of Gujarat, has assured irrigation facility for only 18 lakh hectares or 18% of land, under all the existing schemes. Narmada is the only untopped river, that may provide irrigation to 17.92 lakh hectares of land in 3244 villages. One flower to the garland of Narmada projects is the possible provision of drinking water facility to 131 towns and 4720 villages. The Sardar Sarovar Project is likely to create irrigation potential of 16 lakh hectares, out of which the share of major and medium schemes is 11.55 lakh hectares, 1.74 lakh hectares by way of minor irrigation schemes and 2.70 Lakhs hectares by tube wells.

The advocates of big dams plead that, the launching of the Project may widen the employment base of the economy. Some economists have claimed that, nearly four lakh people will be employed by Narmada project during implementation stage (I.U.B. Reddy).

Table 2

Salient Features of Tehri Dam

Height of the dam	:	260.5 M
Type of the dam	:	Rockfill
Submergence	:	112 Villages and Tehri Township.
Catchment Area	:	6921.25 Sq. K.M.
Power generation	:	600 M.W. (1972)
Installed capacity	:	100 (MW) (1981)
		200 (MW) (1989)
Irrigation	:	2.7 Lakh ha.
Cost (1967)	:	Rs. 126.8 Crores
		Rs. 3000 Crores (1989)

There is substance in the contention that, the Sardar Sarovar Project may facilitate the creation installed capacity of power of 1450 M.W. Power is the accelerator of industrial progress and a promoter of wellbeing of people, when it is used for domestic purpose.

The Tehri Dam Project commends superiority to above specified dams, in so far as it creates Hydel power which has not received the requisite attention by planners of the country. The demand for electricity is lowest during mid night and it may be highest during early evenings. The supply has to match demand or tripping of generators may arise. The problem with Thermal station is that once they start burning coal, they can not be switched off at will. While Thermal power stations can produce "base load", Hydel power comes to the aid of the system at the time of peaking. We can shut off generation from hydel station at will, an act not possible in Thermal Station.

Table 3
Irrigation Profile of Sardar Sarovar Project

S. No.	Major and Medium	Minor (Nos.)	The Wells
1.	Completed 77	4500	3500
2.	In Progress 88	922	400
3.	Envisaged 308	2058	4000

Table 4
Quantum of Land and Number of People facing Submergence at Sardar Sarovar

Unit	Gujarat	Maharashtra	Madhya Pradesh	Total
Villages	19	36	182	237
Families	3322	1357	7500	12180
Population	10593	11000	45000	66593
Forest Land (in Acres)	11168	8541	6756	26465
Irrigated Land (In acres)	4634	3751	19464	27849
Other land (in acres)	2639	3930	25205	31774
Total Land	18441	16222	51425	86088

One bright spot in the body of big dams is the improvement in agricultural progress and crop yield that is likely to follow in the wake of creation and utilisation of irrigation potential. The rosy picture with regard to Narmada Power Project is the possible increase in production of commercial crops, like, sugarcane, cotton and vegetables. The Sardar Sarovar Project, which was estimated to cost Rs. 6,400 crores rupees may increase agricultural income by Rs. 900 crores, the increase in income through electricity will be Rs. 400 crores.

The advocates of Sardar Sarovar Project take no pains to recapitulate the nightmarish droughts of 1987 in Gujarat, which has pushed the wheels of agricultural progress backwards by affecting 77% of Gujarat population and 71% of cropped area in more than 15,000 villages. The silver lining in the cloudy weather is Sardar Sarovar Project.

There is also a widely shared view that, the completion of major dams may set in motion, the train of activities complementary to agriculture viz. animal husbandry, fishery and dairy Industry.

The discussion leads us to the conclusion: Big dam are a blessing for a country.

Section – III

Case Against Major Irrigation Projects

In the present century, environmental degradation has emerged as a global concern for human survival. It is admitted on all hands that, mammoth irrigation projects will submerge villages after installation and tribal population dwelling in village areas would lose their hands. It is unlikely that, appropriate rehabilitation measure will be taken up to atone for the loss involved in the process. Sardar Sarovar Project will totally submerge 37 villages and another 200 villages comprising 1000 families. The sad tune in the song of Narmada Project is submergence of 89 villages fully and partially another 60 villages. It was reasoned by a scholar (Vimal Jhanjari, *India Today*, October 30, 2000 Narmada Valley will uproot lakhs) that neither Gujarat, nor Madhya Pradesh states are in a position to provide the displaced persons in their respective states with alternative agricultural lands.

(i) It must be realised that, rehabilitation is not a mere physical process, it is a psychological process as well and demands adjustment on part of people to novel surroundings. It is doubtful, whether the tribal population living in hilly surroundings can cope with the stresses and strains of rehabilitation. There is a tremendous body of consensus that, tribal population are brought up in an atmosphere of harmony with nature in man-nature interaction process. The heroic legends of Bhagiratha sage will be last after the installation of Teheran Dam. The tribal population have their own methods of recreation like, Pandava dance. Major Dams may close the doors for social harmony.

It is no gainsay that, agriculture and forests are the sole source of sustenance for the tribals. The eviction of these people from their land deprive them of their agricultural lands. The act of refraining them from agriculture and forest based activities may bring natural disaster in their means of livelihood and ways of life.

(ii) There is a body of consensus that, there is under-estimation of cost of construction by the architects of big dams. It is possible that, the costs would rise in all major irrigation projects like Tehri Dam and Narmada Project. Hence, power and irrigation facilities, which were claimed to accrue to people of the area may not be available in proportions as claimed. For instance, the cost of Sardar Sarovar Project, which was estimated to be Rs. 4,240 crores at 1981-82 price level has reached the figure of Rs. 6,406 crores at 1986-87 price level.

(iii) In recent years, doubts about safety have been expressed by many, on account of the fact that, dams are going to be located in the region of high sesimity and hence is risk prove. S.P. Singh in an illumining article captioned Tehri Dam – an assessment (*Yojana*, June 1-15, 1990) beautifully states that, successful behaviour of dams built in high sesimic areas is the singular evidence of the present-day dam technology.

Fresh thinking may be called for before switching on to major dams, because of Reservoir Induced Sesimicity (R.I.S). As and when the Tehri reservoir fills up after the dam is constructed, the load of the water in the reservoir could trigger an earthquake. R.I.S phenomenon emerges in cases where foundation rocks are previous enough to lot water deep through to deep layers of water below. This challenge is met by protagonists of big dam, who argue that, in none of the reservoirs created in Himalayas, Bhakras, Beas, Ramaganaga, R.I.S. has been noted. Even in cases, where R.I.S. has occurred, the trend has been loss than 4 i.e. earth- quakes which are not felt by humans and are incapable of causing any human damage. The internationally known earthquake expert, Pro. Jaikrishna contends that, if at all induced sesimity follows, it is not a design factor but may cause damage to poorly built dwellings, which can be strengthened to reinforce assurance.

(iv) It is plausible to believe that, development economists all over the world clamour for Sustainable Development. Enormous environmental degradation attends the installation of major dams. There is ample statistical evidence to support the view that, the ecology will suffer. The Narmada Sagar Project is likely to submerge 3.5 lakh hectares of India's best decidous forests comprising rich teak and bamboo forests. It seems that, the cost-benefits analysis of scientific and technical personnel may take into account only tangible economic values like, timber and minor Forest produce and discount, invaluable ecologic values like water replenishment, climatic stabilisation and purification and wildlife shelter. Hence, there may be gross under-valuation of Forest loss. In recent years, the Forest Research Institute, Dehradun has estimated the intangible valuation of forests of Narmada at Rs. 14.7 lakh per tree in 50 years. On this basis, the environmental cost of loss of forests in case of Narmada Project would be Rs. 30,293 crores.

(v) It is an established fact that, river valley projects are not a positive proposition in India. Usually a project is sanctioned by Planning Commission only, when the cost–benefit ratio is 1:1.5. Numerous studies at country level have shown that, the cost benefit ratio in case of construction of dams is only 1:0.46. The suggestion, therefore is that, major big dams are not, as beneficial as it is claimed by the proponents of big dams.

There is a body of consenusus that, construction of dams may give rise to sedimentation problem leading to decrease in the life of spans of dams to for below 100 years. Soil erosion and lowering of water tables may conspire together to deteriorate the fertility of soil in the areas close to the Project. Sardar Sarovar Project may submerge 1 Lakh hectores of fertile cotton soil, natural forests and orchards. Besides, 23 K.Ms. of Railway track, 85 K.Ms. of road, 45 K.Ms. of telephone and 19000 buildings will be submerged by Sardar Sarovar Dam.

(vi) Siltation or sedimentation is the serious shortcoming of a dam. There would be deposits of silt in the base of the dam and within few years, the dam may not be capable of supplying water in huge quantities. It goes without saying that, the life span of a dam depends largely on its storage capacity, which in turn depends on the silt load of the river. If silt load exceeds the amount calculated during the planning stage, the storage capacity is gradually diminished and its life-span gets reduced. It has been estimated that, the process of siltation has reduced the water holding capacity of dams of 1.5 to 2.0 per cent per annum. Quite naturally, the life span of a dam gets reduced.

What the critics contend is the possible spread of water-borne disease like, Malaria, headaches and diarrhoea in the adjoining area by the stagnant water of the reservoir.

The disenchantment with the performance of major irrigation works has compelled the former Prime Minister of India, Indira Gandhi to publicly state in her address to State Irrigation Ministers in 1986 "since 1951, 256 big surface irrigation Projects have been initiated, only 65 out these have been completed 181 are still under construction." For 16 years we have poured money out. The People have got nothing back, no irrigation, no water, no increase in production.

Alternatives to Big Dams

In lively debates questions have been raised by scholars of all hues regarding the viability of high dams. The alternatives suggested are construction of a number of smaller dams instead of one dam or smaller structure, which are intended not for storing of water but diversion of flows available in the river at a particular points of time to power or irrigation channels for providing power or irrigation benefits which may be considered as "Run- off the River Schemes".

Academic discussion may pinpoint that to replace a single dam irrigating 1,00,000 ha. 10 small dams, each irrigating 5000 ha. would need to be constructed in upper or lower reaches of water-shed. Such a number of dam sites are seldom available.

Section – IV

The line of reasoning presented in the foregoing paragraph s suggested that, large dams are a mixed blessing. In the context of a search for policy-making it is worth remembering the warnings of Brundtland Commission in "Environment and Development", "World in which poverty is endemic will always be prone to ecological and other catastrophes.

Time and again a pertinent question is being asked should not be water resources of the economy be utilised for the benefit of the entire country? Yes, these, should be utilised in a manner that the adverse effects on the ecosystem are minimised. Minimising adverse effect on large dams on ecosystem due to implementation of projects should be the foremost objectives of planning process at country level. The life of the dam is short. We have to ensure that, the benefits of dam outweigh the demerits of dam.

(1) *Careful Selection of the Resettlement Site*

Conventional widow cautions us to select the resettlement site after taking into account the linking of the affected people. This consideration is essential, because affected people have enormous attachment to soil. Considering people's choice at the time of selection of people's resettlement site may console them at the time of resettlement.

(2) Completion of rehabilitation work should proceeds submergence of villages and catchment area. The arithmetics of Table shows that, 66,593 persons in the States of Gujarat, Maharashtra and Madhya Pradesh will be affected by the Sardar Sarovar Project. The Project will submerge 31,774 acres in Gujarat, Maharashtra, and M.P. Efforts may be made by social activist, Government Official and voluntary agencies to complete rehabilitation work before the lands of the catchment areas are submerged under water. Inordinate delays in implementation of projects as well as rehabilitation work may have adverse effects on the economy and should be avoided.

(3) Payment of compensation to people in instalments. People should be educated and motivated to productively utilise money. So, instead of paying money at a time, pecuniary assistance may be given to people in instalments, so that people realise after spending some amount, about its utilisation.

(4) *Provision of Cultivable Lands to Affected Persons*

Promotion of welfare of human beings is the be-all and end all of development. Towards, the end, following the completion of Sardar Sarovar Project, Gujarat Government has provided two hect. of land to 800 Project Affected Person (PAP) from Gujarat and 159 (PAP)s from Maharashtra. All these lands are neither waste nor forest, these are already in cultivation in common area. It is heartening to note that, 800 families in Gujarat are also provided with residential plots, subsistence allowance, subsidy for bullocks, bullock carts, civic amenities and insurance cover. Such welfare support measures should form an integral part of Policy-making, while considering installation of a project in an area.

(5) Creation of alternative employment generating schemes like J.R.Y, P.M's Rojgar Yojana should be accorded top priority.

(6) Investment in Training and Skill Upgradation of People.

People are the non-material capital of a country. People who are benefit of their livelihood, due to project installation should be given suitable training in non-traditional works.

Cost-benefit analysis of projects should consider not only economic costs but also social costs of the project. One sinister aspect of plan performance in India is that, the actual utilisation of irrigation potential by the economy lags behind the irrigation potential already created by the economy.

Conclusion

To conclude, major dams have both the sides, brighter side as well as darker side. We want development through dams, which do not destroy environment. The execution of major river valley projects may be reduced to the minimum. Focus may be laid on cost effective small dams and minor irrigation works, which reduce water-logging and salinity. Successful execution of river valley projects depends on employment of displaced person in suitable lines, appropriate settling of rehabilitation persons and provision of land and cash payment to affected persons. All this requires collective wisdom of planner, irrigation experts and socially oriented persons. Above all, environmental clearance of river valley projects is an indispensable necessity while approving the project.

Dedication

The article is dedicated to the memory of my father-in-law late V.M.A. Rama Rao, Advocate and advisor, Jaganath Mandir, Koraput.

REFERENCES

1. Dr. Vidyut Joshi, "Sardar Sarovar Project: Thesis, Anti-thesis and synthesis", *Yojana*, June, 1-15, 1990.
2. Arabind Ghose, Tehri Dam Project – A harbinger of prosperity; *Yojana*, June 1-15, 1990.

3. S.P. Singh, "Tehri Dam – An assessment and a vision", *Yojana*, June, 1-15, 1990.
4. I.U.B. Reddy, "Cost of River Valley in India". *Indian Journal of Public Administration*, Vol. 35, No. 3, 1989.
5. The Hindu 28, 29.11.2000.
6. I.U.B. Reddy, "Narmada Multipurpose Project. Boonorbane". *Yojana* April 19-30, 1988.
7. Rudar Dutt & K.P.M. Sundaram, *Indian Economy*. Sultan Chand & Co., 2001.
8. *India Today* "Narmada Dam – The Final. October 20, 2000.
9. Sanat Meheta, "Sardar Sarovar Project: An overview" *Yojana*, June 1-15, 1990.

6

Land Acquisition for Development Projects and Rehabilitation of Displaced Persons (A Case Study of NALCO, Orissa)

— *Dr. C.R. Das**

To execute various development projects very often entails acquisition of various type of land with the acquisition of every piece of land by the project authority in the name of national interest/public purpose on which many people have been living since past many generations and property as well as common property resources like pasture land, burial ground, religious places, educational institutions, roads and bridges etc. On which their day to day socio-economic religious and cultural life attached they have been establishing since their birth. The land which provide them their life sustenance food, fodder medicine etc. not only a status symbol of owners or income generating asset but its value is more than their price as their life system attached to it.

In course of time, the increase in population density and declining per capita availability of land as result of break down of joint family system acquisition of land for development/ national interest in most cases in resulting is displacement of human settlement from their native habitat. The expropriation of land with legal coerce make the native habitat of face unnatural disaster. The devastation due to loss of land causes

* *Economic Research Supervisor, N.K.C. Centre for Development Studies, Bhuneshwar (Orissa).*

break down of the recycling system of income, employment, livelihood, disruption in social relationship, deviating from the age old religious cultural factors need to be addressed properly.

To materialisc the plan for over all development in Orissa, large and variety number of projects have been launched to exploit unutilised natural resources. For such development induced projects large extent of area of land have been acquired. In the process of land acquisition, a large number of people affected in different degrees. A large chance of families have been uprooted losing their name and health as well as shattering their culture whereas others lost their livelihood resources and occupation which has been built over several generations. From 1950 to 1993 a total number of 85,510 families have been displaced presented in the Table 1 below:

Table 1
Displaced Families due to Development Projects in Orissa from 1950-1993

Categories of Projects	No. families offered	Percentage of total displacement
1. Mines	3143	3.7
2. Industries	10704	12.5
3. Thermal Power Plant	2426	2.8
4. Dam Projects	64903	75.9
5. Wild Life Sanctuary	142	0.2
6. Urban Slums Clearance	4792	4.9
Total	85510	100.0

These figure in Table 1 reveals that for dam project highest number of families displaced followed by industrial as the table is simple and self-explanatory.

It is the prime responsibility of the Government and the executing agencies to restore the living standard of displaced persons, who sacrificed for a greater national interest through proper resettlement and rehabilitation. Till 1973, the displaced and project affected families were only paid cash compensation for value of their land property acquired. But peoples movement and resistance compelled the Government and project authorities to extended liberal and lucrative Resettlement and Rehabilitation measures to assist the affected people along with the cash compensation.

It is found that the displaced persons of most of the development projects were unable to socially rearticulate in the resettlement sites. The host population in the relocation sites not treated equally to those displaced persons, who have been suffering without any fault of them. Again the benefits provided for extention of all type of supports to them too. Therefore, private and public sector undertakings are extended to all those living in the nearby villages/area under the purview of peripheral development programme (PDP). The integrated approach bring socio-economic benefit for both displaced persons and persons living in nearby areas through providing better infrastructure facilities in order to improve their road and communication, educational, health, drinking water facilities which in turn help to push up their living standard upward. Such investment also provide employment and encome to the local people.

Legal Aspects of Land Acquisition

Land acquisition is on the concurrent list of the Indian Constitution. Land is normally acquired under the provisions of the Land Acquisition Act, 1894 which is a general and basic law in the country for the acquisition of land for public purposes and for exploring unutilised natural resources to push up the standard of living of our country people. This act was comprehensively amended in the year 1984, taking into consideration the recommendations of the Law Commission, Land Acquisition Review Committee headed by Shri A.N. Mulla, MP, as well as suggestions from the State Governments and other quarters. The Land Acquisition Act, 1894 is a Statutory Statement of the State's power of eminent domain, which vests the state with ultimate control over land within its territory. For instance in 1994, in the case of Ram Chand *Vs* Union of India (ISCC 44, pp 49-50) the Supreme Court observed that 'The power to acquire private property for public use is an attribute of sovereignty and is essential to the existence of a government.' The power of eminent domain was recognized on the principle that the sovereign state can always acquire the property of a citizen for public good, without the owner's consent. Therefore, land can either be purchased directly or acquired through only of the relevant Legislations created by the Central or State Governments. The land requirements of public or major private sector projects are met through the Land Acquisition Act, 1894 and its Section 16, stipulates that when the district Collector has made an award under section 11 of the Act, he or she may take possession of the land, which shall there upon vest absolutely in the government, free from all incumbencies. The owner thereafter compulsorily loses his right, title and interest to the land in return for a cash compensation declared under the terms of the award.

As majority of our mineral resources, including coal, iron ore, and manganese reserves are located in the remote and backward regions mostly inhabited by tribals. Those land area required for industrial and mega power projects, large scale construction of multi- purpose irrigation dams, mining operations, reservation of forests and creation of sanctuaries, National Parks, construction of canals, highways and transmission lines and land required for construction roads and buildings to develop infrastructure of the country. This is aimed at overall development of unutilised resources to strengthen the economic backbone of our country.

In case of large scale displacement due to land acquisition in tribal areas cash compensation alone has not been acceptable to them, then it has become the practice to provide job/ employment at the rate of one person per family in addition to cash compensation. Additional benefits like developed or semi-developed house sites, shifting allowances, preferential employment of the other members of the project displaced persons were declared as resettlement packages with different norms being followed at different places and undertakings.

In February 1986, the Bureau of Public Enterprises instructed that any understanding, formal or informal, in regard to the offer of employment to one member of ever dispossessed family in the project, will stand withdrawn. This further restricted the scope of rehabilitation programmes. The Land Acquisition Act is no isolated in its relevance to displacement. The Forest Act, 1927, which anticipated the displacement of people from Forests in which the state declared an interest. The Maneuvers, Field. Firing and Artillery Practice Act, 1938 states total "exclusion or removed from any place declared to be a danger zone of persons or domestic animals in the 'interests of safety'. The Railway Act, 1989 enable State authorities to take over control of land and related resources for the purpose of constructing of maintaining a railway, or to construct in or upon, across, under or over any lands or any streets, hills, valleys, roads, railways town way" as it thinks proper. But the conference of the Revenue Secretaries of State which was held in July 1989 has recommended that all lands should be acquired under the provisions of the Land Acquisition Act, 1894 alone and other laws repugnant there to should be amended or repealed altogether (Government of India, 1989). The Land Acquisition Amendment Act, 1984 while being a step in the right direction to bring about a rapprochement between the interests of the displaced land owners and those of the state, failed to offer a comprehensive solution to the problems of all sections of the displaced population.

The failure of administration and project authorities to protect the legitimate interest of the people living in interior areas, specially tribals due to (a) absence or incompleteness of record of rights of land utilised by tribals since time immemorial and (b) non-measurement of their dependence on common property resources like, forest and other government land which provide substantial part of their livelihood.

In addition to the wide spread displacement of population, the projects will also cause loss of vast tracts of arable and forest lands. It is estimated that the country is loosing 1.5 to 2.5 million hectares of good land every year due to initiation of various projects (TRTI, 1987). What is more disturbing feature of displacement is that in a rural agricultural economy/traditional forest depending communities land is not only a site–it is the prime means of production and life sustaining source. In case of agricultural land it supports the owner, his servants, agricultural labourers, the village artisans, the merchants who buys the produce and a host of others acting in such a system. Similarly the forest and other village common land such as pasture land, graveyard or religious place attached with economic, social, cultural and religious fabric of village society collapsed with the displacement by acquisition of land which diverted for a more important use as perceived by the Government. When the cycle of agriculture and allied activities are disturbed all other backward and forward activities bearing linkages to these activities and on which households were depending for their livelihood also endangered which was including those resourceless and landless people. The Land Acquisition Act does not provide any benefits for such people.

NALCO–POST DISPLACEMENT CONDITIONS AT DAMANJODI

Background

The fifth largest deposit of Bauxite of the world discovered in Koraput district of Orissa during late 1970s compelled Government of India to consider for establishing an Integrated Bauxite-Alumina–Aluminium Complex in the state. The quest for exploitation of such huge amount of natural resources led to the signing of a memorandum of understanding for initiating discussions on technical collaboration and financing of one of the largest integrated aluminium projects of the world, with a French Corporation with the presence of the President of France in January 1980. In November, 1980, Government of India sanctioned the establishment of the Orissa Aluminium Complex which was christened and registered as National Aluminium Company Limited (NALCO) on 7th January, 1981.

The then Prime Minister of India, late Smt. Indira Gandhi had laid down the foundation stone of NALCO at Damanjodi on 27th March 1981. Which was a gigantic Indo-French Flag Project. While she had laid down the foundation stone, she declared that NALCO would strive to realise the better quality of life of not only displaced persons but also the tribal people living in and around the area. The Integrated Aluminium Complex has two main segments in Koraput district, i.e. (1) Bauxite mines in the Panchpatmali with a deposit of 112.8 million tonnes in Damanjodi with potential capacity of production 24 lakhs ton per year, (2) Aluminium Refinery with 8 lakh ton per year, (3) Aluminium plant at Angul with 2.18 lakh ton per year supported by Captive Power plant of 600 MW and (4) for export marketing of alumina of 3.75 lakh ton per year port facilities provided at Visakhapatnam. The Bauxite mine at Panchpatmali estimated to provide raw materials for over 100 years, deposited ore in 16 square kilometer area (20 KM length and 0.8 kilometre average width). The quality of ore are consisting of 45 per cent of Alumina and 2 per cent of silica. For establishment of NALCO at Damanjodi land acquired area and the status of land, compensation paid upto 31.1.2001 are presented in the Table 2.

From the above table it is revealed that at Damanjodi for NALCO Government of Orissa acquired land area of 7262.94 acres of land. Of the total land 4532.51 acres of land was of private persons and 2730.43 acres of land was of Government. The land area acquired from private land owner's constituted 62.41 per cent of total land and 37.59 per cent of total land area was forest land (122.91 acres) and non forest government land was 35.90 per cent (2607.53 acres) Private land owners were paid Rupees 15800.88 lakh as compensation for parting with their land whereas Government of Orissa got only Rs. 32.78 lakhs for leasing out of 2730.43 acres of forest as well as non forest land.

Table 2
Status of Land Acquired and Compensation Paid by NALCO Damanjodi as on 31. 1. 2001

Status of Land	Area (in Acres)	Compensation Paid (Rs. in lakhs)
1. Private Land including Basti land	4532.51 (62.41)	15800.88
2. Government Land of which	2730.43 (37.59)	32.78
(a) Forest land	122.91 (1.69)	
(b) Non-Forest land	2607.52 (35.90)	
Total	7262.94 (100.00)	15833.66

Land area acquired both from private land owners and government land measuring 7262.94 acres transferred to NALCO. Land utilised for various purposes deal in above Table 3. Red mud pond of NALCO occupied highest area of 2549.25 acres which is 35.10 per cent of total area followed by development of township which utilised 29.64 per cent of total area of land.

Initially the Displaced Persons (DPs) agitated against the project itself slowly the gave up the agitation as they were of the opinion that what late Smt. Indira Gandhi as a Prime Minister decided for land, jobs and better resettlement though primarily neglected by the project authorities, were compelled to take decision to give unskilled jobs and raise compensation amount to the DPs due to direct intervention of the then Prime Minister Late Indira Gandhi to ensure better compensation and rehabilitation package for DPs.

The work was ceased at Damonjodi, NALCO due to agitation by DPs and as a result the project lost several crores of rupees in foreign exchange on Euro Dollar loans in order to save the additional Rs. 60 lakh that the Project affect people (PAP) were demanding as compensation. One estimate puts the loss at Rs. 35 lakh a day paid in foreign currency as interest on the Euro-Dollar loans. Ultimately, the additional amount required for rehabilitation and resettlement had to be spent, but during the agitation period which stalled the work were causing a avoidable loss of several crores in foreign exchange. However, the tribals and those who were dependent on common property resources (CPRs) were by and large unhappy as their life supporting system lost due to loss of CPR which was unacceptable for them. For loss of CPR neither viable alternative source was available nor compensation paid for such persons in any other way, which lead to marginalisation of such families.

Table 3

Land Utilisation of NALCO at Damanjodi

(Land in Acres)

	Govt. Land	Private Land	Total	Percent of Total Land
a. Alumina plant	578.10	1138.72	1716.82	23.64
b. Red mud pond	1074.79	1474.46	2549.25	35.10
c. Conveyor belt	439.04	123.15	562.19	7.74
d. Township	597.13	1554.69	2151.82	29.63
e. Pipeline	1.77	65.56	67.33	0.93
f. Permanent Water intake	1.89	12.92	14.81	0.20
g. Rehabilitation Colony	----	54.25	54.25	0.75
h. Approach Road	33.60	100.17	133.77	1.84
i. Mines Approach	3.50	3.63	7.13	0.10
j. Mines Lease Camp	0.61	4.96	5.57	0.08
Total	2730.43 (37.59)	4532.51 (62.41)	7262.94	100.00 (100.00)

Development induced displacement of loss of land which results in the marginalisation and impoverishment of the DPs/PAPs particularly of the weaker and illiterate unskilled CPR dependent persons and people who were depend on such a system of serving as agricultural labourers or survivors of traditional occupation were the worst sufferers. The breakdown of social system established since time immemorial due to displacement taken away their life sustaining source of many which forced to climb down from their living standard on one hand where as those PAPs secured a job and ensured good amount of earning push up their living standard on the other. As a result, the gap between them increased at a higher speed which clearly visible in their village community. Even within a family which nominate one person for employment, whose standard of living is far better than the others who are now otherwise unemployed or partly depend on other source of earning which create social tension and break down of well knitted social fabric of the earlier system.

The project authorities categorised the persons who have lost land by way of acquisition by NALCO into 3 categories viz. (1) Local Displaced Persons/Families)LPD) who have lost their land and homestead; (2) Substained Affected Persons/ Families (SAP) who have lost upto 2/3rd of their land holding; (3) Least Affected Persons/Families (LAP) who have lost less than 1/3rd of their total holding.

There has been expectation from the families and family members for absorption in NALCO by way of direct employment. When the concept of 'Person' and not the family (at the time. of land acquisition) becomes the expectant beneficiary the number increase. With breaking down of the joint family system also the concept of family as also family's land holding changes, so also their categorisation into the 3 categories of project affected persons as defined by NALCO. The pressure on NALCO for providing direct employment as also other income generating avocations is continuously increase. Therefore, it is pertinent to note that how the project affected persons resettled and rehabilitated present in the Table 4.

In the table which spell out the rehabilitation and resettlement of project affected persons (PAP) due to NALCO project at Dama- njodi is a self explanatory. There are twelve villages already affected by the project, two villages partially affected are Charanguli and Marichamal and another two villages namely Champa Padar and Khoraguda awaited for eviction from their households. There are 600 families affected by the NALCO of which 522 families are resettled which is 87 per cent of total affected families. As a result of rehabilitation package measure 486 persons from 486 PAP families constituting 81 per cent were secured employment in NALCO, Damanjodi and 114 families yet to secure a job. For one of their family member constitute 19 per cent of toal PAP families.

Table 4

Resettlement and Rehabilitation of Land Displaced Persons at Milling and Refinery Complex, Damanjodi

Sl.No	Name of the Village	No. of Families Affected	No.of Families Resettled	No of Persons Employed	No.of Persons yet to be Employed
1.	Damanjodi	156	155	140	16
2.	Goudayada Hamlet of Damanjodi	20	20	20	–
3.	Goudaguda Hamlet of Ambagam	05	05	05	
4.	Barangaput	20	20	19	1
5.	Patiasil	18	18	16	2
6.	Surriguda	28	28	28	
7.	Kantaguda	60	60	58	2
8.	Mali Dumuriguda	83	83	75	8
9.	Gadipabli	52	52	52	
10.	Surgiguda Hamlet village of Denga Janiguda	06	06	04	2
11.	Jhadiguda	15	15	14	1
12.	Sindhipar	60	60	52	8
13.	Charanguli	01	–	01	
14.	Moricha Mal	01	–	01	
15.	Champa Padar	59	–	01	58
16.	Khoraguda	16	–	–	16
		600 (100.00)	522 (87.00)	486 (81.00)	114 (19.00)

NB: Figures in parentheses represent per cent to total.

Source: NALCO Corporate Office, Bhubaneswar.

Therefore, Reddy (1992) concluded that the panorama of existing rehabilitation could have been better, if the project authorities had drawn up programmes backed up by efficient planning of course industrialisation has raised improved health, education, and housing facilities for a limited number of affected peopled and contributed to a growing consciousness of materialism. All hazards and disadvantages to the project oustee households to be avoided or kept with in tolerance limits as far as possible. Without proper care and effective rehabilitation the very reason for development will lost its fragance. Therefore, the National Policy of Rehabilitation is argued to keep the project affected persons (PAP) not in worst atmosphere.

Environmental Pollution and Control

There are major environmental problems associated with bauxite alumina operations. The mining of bauxite as is the case with the NALCO operations—is generally open cast mining. In case of NALCO, it is entirely mechanised. After trees and shrubs are cleared with bulldozers, over burden is stripped. Stripping ratio can be as high as 15 meters over burden to one meter ore. The over burden is stock piled. Conservation of surface soil that had stock piled is most important to prevent it being washed away in rain water. The ore is loosened with the help of explosives, thereafter excavation is carried out with machineries and stock is transported to conveyor belts on overhead ropeways and bucket, after washing and drying shifted to alumina refinery.

The critical areas of environmental management are (1) Ore mining causing disturbances of land itself, soil erosion, mine run off water, dislocation of the water balance, generation of dust moist and fumes. Spread of diseases and disturbance of natural economic systems and disturbances caused by the creation of infrastructure (2) site rehabilitation (3) environmental management of alumina plants and (4) residue disposal all should be taken care to prohibit unhealthy atmosphere. Further, open cast mining which can generate 0.25 Kg. dust per metric tonne of bauxite mined, stock piles and loading and drying operations.

From the outset of the project, NALCO had adopted anti-pollution and energy efficient state of art of technology. From the design stage single multi curve down hill conveyor equipped with power regeneration system in the bauxite mines, Atmospheric pressure digestion, fluidised bed calciner and generation of power from process stream in the alumina refinery regulated the pollution to a considerable extent. The design of the plant and equipment has been so engineered that there is no pollution of water and air but disposal of waste and industrial residual management should be strictly implemented.

Besides planting more than 6 million trees NALCO has been spent more than 100 crores on equipment and facilities for treatment of effluent containing dust, reducing noise levels and for holding the ash and red mud slurry in ponds. With the advent of new technology, it should be installed so that pollution control should be further reduced upto the extent not to affect the persons living in its periphery area in particular and to our environment and ecology in general.

Periphery Development

Displaced families of most of the development projects have failed to socially rearticulate in the relocation sites. The families also living in nearby villages and affected due to its installation also aspiring to get some support and benefits for a better atmosphere. Therefore, peripheral development programme has been launched to contain the hostility of nearby affected villages by extending various facilities and services. Most of the development programmes those have been undertaken to improve socio-economic conditions of the people living in its periphery includes development of infrastructure and communication, improvement of health and sanitation system, providing better educational infrastructure, and protection of socio-cultural values etc. Nearby villages affected due to installation of NALCO at Damanjodi also benefitted due to its periphery development works. For a better understanding a table is presented below showing the amount of rupees has been spent on various since inception of 1999-2000.

Table 4
Periphery Development Works undertaken by NALCO, Damanjodi

(Amount in lakhs)

S.N	Scheme	Upto 1990	1991-93	1994-96	1997-98	1998-99	1999-2000	Total
1.	Drinking Water	17.17	31.04	67.21	1.00	3.60	1.40	93.484
2.	Health and Sanitation	–	–	50.37	2.50	11.50	11.40	75.77 (8.62)
3.	Education	12	2.995	7.90	11.00	3.10	11.00	47.995 (5.46)
4.	Housing	89.20	–	15.66	–	–	–	104.86 (11.93)
5.	Infrastructure and Communication	300.88	6.71	69.575	16.00	37.50	71	501.665 (57.07)
6.	Agriculture and Allied	1.23	1.165	2.30	–	–	2.00	6.695 (0.76)
7.	Socio–Cultural	9.08	2.89	–	20.50	8.15	8.00	48.62 (5.53)
	Total	429.56 (48.86)	16.804 (1.92)	213.015 (24.23)	51.00 (58.0)	63.85 (7.26)	104.8 (11.93)	879.00 (100.00)

(Figures in parentheses represent per cent to total.)
Source: NALCO, Corporate Officer, Bhubaneswar.

Under periphery development programme 879.09 lakhs of rupees has been spent since its inception, but of total amount has been spent so far expenditure on infrastructure and communication development programmes is around Rs. 5 crore which is 57.07 per cent. The share of expenditure till now on housing under periphery development scheme is 11.93 per cent followed by Drinking water 10.63 per cent, health and sanitation 8.62 per cent, socio-cultural 5.53 per cent, education 5.46 per cent and for agriculture and allied activities only 0.76 per cent of total fund diverted and utilised since inception to till now. There should be a policy guide line to divert a specific percent and amount for general welfare in the schemes like health, drinking water, education and generation of income and employment for local people under peripheral development programmes.

Conclusion

NALCO, no doubt, has been undertaking a number of measures for cessation of hostility attitude of displaced persons (DPs) and project affected persons (PAPs). Various studies also have undertaken to evaluate the achievement, study the reaction of PAPs and implementing and execution the recommendation of experts. Besides, peripheral development programmes, which considerably enhance the standard of living of middle class and higher socio-economic groups. Landless labourers and dependent households on CPRs particularly Forest Dependent households unable to exploit the opportunity and suffer a lot, to be provided with special care by the Project authorities. Further considering from the point of view of gender issues, lower class women who were earning regularly from their work based on traditional system of agriculture and primary forest produce gathering lost their perennial sources of income and livelihood without proper alternative arrangement to suit their labour. To help such persons the project authority should undertake programmes to provide them necessary training on dairying, poultry farming, gardening, knitting, tailoring etc. And provide necessary asset like cows, buffaloes, poultry birds, machinery and tools as per primary requirements for carrying our such work. For sustainable development they should by organise on co-operative basis to look after their own business.

NALCO, the gigantic corporate sector in India should be more effective in discharging its social responsibility by providing necessary infrastructure and facilities to its DPs/PAPs whose sacrifice at the primary stage turn the dream Project successful on today.

REFERENCES

1. Carnea, Michael, M. (1990), From unused social knowledge to policy creation: The case of population Resettlement, Development Discussion Paper No. 342, Harvard University, USA.
2. Ministry of Rural Development, Government of India, 'Draft National Policy for Rehabilitation of Persons Displaced as a consequence of Acquisition of Land.
3. Reddy, I.U.B. (1992): *Displacement and Rehabilitation*, Mittal Publications, New Delhi.
4. Srinivasan, Kannan; Vyasulu, 'The Orissa Aluminium Complex Points towards a Debate', in Vinod, Rajagopalan, S. (1981): *EPW* XVI (49), PP 2005-2014.
5. Subrahmanyam, K.V. (1982), Orissa Aluminium Complex, *EPW*, XVII (5) pp. 168-172.
6. Tribal Research and Training Institute, Poona, (1987): Displacement of Tribals due to Location of Central/State Projects: Problems and Related Issues. *Tribal Research Bulletin* 9 (2) : 21-26

7

Displacement and Development: The Land Acquisition Act 1894 (As Amended in 1984): A Critical Review with Special Reference to Orissa

— *Dr. G. B. Nath**

Displacement of people from their habitat occurs almost in all countries due to the provision for infrastructural public utilities like hydroelectric complexes, irrigation canals, exploration of minerals and industrial centres etc. Payment of compensation for the property so acquired possess a formadible problem for the authority acquiring them. In recent years a good deal of studies are available highlighting among other things, the problem of valuation and payment of compensation for the assets. In almost all the projects that have acquired land the common complaint is the under valuation of the land and other assets by the land acquisition authority and payment of inappropriate compensation. Even the funding authority like World Bank has recognised the problem of incorrect assessment of compensation for the acquired assets. Presently the problem of land acquisition and payment of compensation is handled the colonial Land Acquisition Act 1894 (as amended in 1984). The present paper is a critique of the L.A. Act with special reference to Orissa. The paper argues that the L.A. Act 1894 as has been amended in 1984 is full of anomalies and contradictions. Hence, it has made the land acquisition

---

* *Reader and Head, Department of Economics, L.N. College, Jharsuguda (Orissa)-768202.*

procedure a complex one and prohibits the payment of fair compensation to the project oustees. The operation of the said act has given the authority of the state to abuse power and fix the rate of compensation in a most arbitrary manner. Hence there is a need for the repeal of the said colonial act and replace it with an acceptable and democratic land acquisition act.

History of the Land Acquisition Act (1894)

On the eve of modernising Calcutta by the then seat of Power of Imperial Government there was a need for the construction of wide roads and communication systems. However, this cannot be accomplished without acquiring the rights of the individual over their land. Therefore the then Indian Legislature made several attempts at legislation for providing for compulsory acquisition of land and payment of compensation on them. Consequently the first All India Act VI of 1857 was passed where owners of land may be required by the legislature to surrender some of their rights they possess over their land for purposes of public utility.

Subsequently a well defined, all comprehensive Land Acquisition Act, covering the whole of British India came into force on the first day of March 1894 as the Act 1 of 1894. Till now with minor amendments this Act is being followed by the State as well as Central Government in India in the matter of acquisition of land and distribution of compensation to the oustees (Venkataraman 1938).

Main Provisions of the 1894 Land Acquisition Act (L.A. Act)

The Land Acquisition Act 1894 consists of eight parts and fifty-five sections, each chapter dealing with a category of provision and the sections and subsections explaining and clarifying the provisions. Below are the main provisions of the Act.

The L.A. Act 1894 authorises the government to acquire land compulsorily for the government or for a company or for any public purpose. It is 'Public purpose' which determines whether the land should be acquired or not and consideration of individual hardship can never out-weight the question of public demand. However, a person interested in the land that would be acquired, shall be heard on his objection if made in writing within 30 days of the notification. The Collector, if necessary would make an enquiry and then make a reference to the local government with a report containing his recommendations. After considering the report of the Collector that any particular land is needed for public purpose or for a company, a declaration would be made that the land has been acquired for public purpose. After the declaration, the Collector would arrange for the land to be marked out, measured and notices would be given to the persons interested on the land and makes the award of the compensation in respect of the land acquired and then the Collector would take possession of the land so acquired.

However, the Collector has been empowered to take immediate possession of waste or arable land in case of urgency although no award of compensation had been made, provided he has obtained the previous sanction of the local government for such immediate occupation. Of course the opinion of the government on the nature of the urgency is unquestionable.

Valuation and Payment of Adequate Compensation

The provision of the Act provides for the valuation of the land to be acquired and payment of adequate compensation to the legal owner of the property. While assessing the compensation money, section 23 of the Act enumerates the matters to be considered in determining the compensation amount like (1) the market value of the land, (2) damage substained by the person interested and (3) by taking of any standing crops trees, or other type of damage suffered by the individual agrived.

Similarly Section 24 of the Act provides for certain factors which should not be taken into consideration in determining the compensation like (1) the degree of urgency, (2) any dis-inclination on the part of the owner, (3) any damage sustained by a third party, (4) any damage which is likely to be caused to the land acquired, (5) any increase to the value of the land acquired or likely to accrue from the use to which it will be put when acquired, (6) any increase to the value of the other lands of the claimant, and (7) any outlay or improvement on or dispose of the land after the declaration.

A Critical Appraisal of the Legislation

To repeat the main feature of the Act put together were: the individual has got the property right or ownership which can be acquired by the State and while acquiring it the state would pay adequate compensation. In each and every case of acquisition of the property the element of public purpose is quite crucial in the Act.

The Act, thus, carries in principle the hereditary right to property of an individual and tries to make us believe that the right of the state is superior to that the right of the individual. This is why the state can take away the property of any individual at any time of course for the "Public purpose".

However the term "Public purpose" used in the Act is not defined. In the absence of a proper guideline so as to the definition of the term public purpose makes the application of the whole act an arbitrary one (Rao 1995). For anything can be put by the government under the banner of public purpose to acquire land. Moreover the Collector of a district has been given the absolute authority to determine what is public purpose and what is not.

One interesting reading of the Act is that an affected person by the acquisition of the land cannot even question the decision of the Collector on the element of "Public purpose" in the acquisition of the land, though he can go to the court of law questioning the amount of compensation, the area acquired, etc.

Even though land has been taken for a genuine public purpose then the question of compensation remains. The guiding factor for the act to determine the compensation is market value of land considering the sale and purchase deed of the locality, sale of the neighbouring lands, opinions of the experts, previous award, expected rates of return from the land etc. Thus the Act does not define the term market value and there is a consequential arbitrariness in determining the compensation rate. For example when a land has been recently purchased, the purchase money would be the best evidence of its market value. However land which were situated in much interior parts where there is no such sale or purchase it is difficult to ascertain on the basis of the produce or by means of recent sale it can be determined on the sale or similar lands in the neighbourhood. The price paid within a reasonable time for land adjacent to the land acquired and possessing similar advantages in considered to be a correct method of valuation.

The usual practice that is followed for valuation of the compensation on land is based on the quality of land possessed by the oustees. But the quality based pricing of land may not provide fair compensation to the oustees due to (1) The usual practice to show lower price of the land by the buyers of the land in the registered sale deeds with a view to avoid stamp duty, (2) Tendency of the people to record their fertile land as low grade land to pay less land revenue to the state and (3) Most of the project oustees have encroached the forest lands and cultivating them for generations for which there is no legal records or pattas and consequently they are not entitled to receive compensation for these lands. Furthermore in a semifeudal setup where monetisation is in a low scale and the ownership, control and operation of the landed property is concentrated in few hands, a market for land would be conspicuous in its absence. Thus there could not be any free, and competitive market for the land. Thus the idea of land as a market may not be there in the minds of the people. In such a situation the treatment of land as commodity become a purchasers market and not a sellers market. Therefore the party acquiring the land will be in a upper hand to dictate the price in the deal and this would put the later in more trouble if the acquiring agency is the state. When Government acquires land forcefully, fair and adequate compensation is a misnomor.

The real problem with the Act starts when the amount of compensation has been settled under section II, and any dispute arises as to the apportionment. Thus the Act directs the Collectors under section 30 and refers such a dispute to the decision of the court. When the apportionment is between the landlords and tenants consisting of the tenants at will or subtenants or even in case of occupancy tenants it is the landlord to gain and the tenant who will loose in the drawn legal battle between them. In an economy where the tenants right are in a underdeveloped stage and there is a large number of heirarical claimants to the land it is the tiller of the soil who would be the real sufferer in receiving the compensation money. The Act does not provides any compensation to a propertyless tenants at will, share cropper, agricultural labourers. The basic features of the Act is to compensate the person who is loosing the property in the process of acquisition of land. It does not go into the question of a person who is loosing his source of living due to the forceful acquisition of the land in which he was making a living by hiring his labour. Thus while land acquisition has a legal standing, rehabilitation has no legal standing. A person who has been deprived of his means of livelihood has no legal remedy for rehabilitation (Rao 1995).

However, it is interesting to note that the primary thrust of the L.A. Act is to quicken the process of land acquisition but not to mediate on the right over land. Therefore it was not surprising that people having the right over lands were rehabilitated and compensated but people having inferior right were thrown up. Thus the evolution of the legal structure is such that it strengthens the pre-capitalist social order along with creation of a proletarianised section of the society. Corroborative evidences can be found out from a number of studies on displaced persons from sites of projects for big dams, thermal and nuclear power stations, military projects, big industries and mining operations etc. all over India by the concerned scholars. These projects have destablished the material base of the tribals, have dethroned them from their habitats, and marginalised them. Thus capital penetration for that matter 'development' has not integrated the marginalised section into the capitalistic frame work but has alienated them from it.

Implementation of the Act

Pandit Jawaharlal Nehru came to lay the foundation stone of the Hirakud Dam Project on April 12, 1948.[1] In his speech he promised to the people of the area that land for land and house for house would be given and no body would be made destitute. In 1948 Government of Orissa passed a Special Act (Act 18 of 1948) in accordance with the Land Acquisition Act 1 of 1894 in order to expedite the process of acquisition of land for the Hirakud Dam Project.

However the reality was something different. The incredible rate of payment compensation came to light when the first land acquisition started in the village 'Jamanda' for the Hirakud Dam workshop on an area of 27 acres and 76 decimals with a total amount of compensation amounted to Rs. 519.50 or Rs. 18 and 12 annas per acres or 3 annas per decimal on the average.[2] It was learnt that the possession of the land was taken on 2nd April 1948 and after one year the payment of compensation was made on 14th April, 1949 at the above rate. Again no promise of land for land and house for house was kept by the government. Twenty-four families from Jamanda did not get adequate compensation, nor did they offered with land elsewhere. As a matter of fact not a single square inch of land was reclaimed till February 1949.[3]

By the rainy season of 1955-69 villages were to be evacuated for filling up part of the reservoir. So about four thousand families were evacuated with the help of military policy by the summer if 1955. Most of them had not received any compensation by that time. Evidently, those who had received nothing could afford to get any land either in the government reclamation centres or purchase lands elsewhere. When the reservoir was filled up fully for the first time during the rainy season of 1956 people evacuated during summer after route march by millitary police in the remaining 180 villages covering an area of 743 square kilometers were submerged kicking out more than 15 thousand families. However till 25.9.56 1410[4] (or 9.4 per cent of the total) families could be settled in the government resettlement centres. The area submerged was 1 lakh 47 thousand and 363 acres. In exchange the people got only 3 thousand 790 acres less than 3 per cent of land.[5] It was aleged that since in Sambalpur the real tenants have little right over their land they could not get much compensation.[6]

By utilising the Land Acquisition Act 1948 the Orissa the Gountia, Zamindars or proprietors could able to get whatever benefits was accruing to them most of them also could fight with the state in legal battle and have owned certain concessions. The net loss of the tenants, sharecroppers and agricultural labourers were enormous.

The foundation stone for the Rengali Multi-purpose Dam Project was laid down by the then Prime Minister Indira Gandhi on 23rd December 1973. The reservoir submerged 4,14,500 hac. of land. One of the village study of 104 households show that majority of the households are unaware of the compensation criteria fixed by the project authority. Cultivators those who are cultivating the 'encroachment' land for which the 'Patta' or record of right was not given by the revenue authority did not get any compensation for these lands. There was also no uniformity in the payment of compensation. The proportied section belonging to the rich peasants and landlord social category became better off compared to the non-propertied social groups belonging to the poor peasants and agricultural labour households in term of compensation (Nath 1984) some of the dissatisfied households approached by the court. However, the judgement of higher compensation does not apply automatically to the other affected households who does not approach the court. Some households were not sure of getting the judgement, in their favour and their poverty debar them for going to the court by paying the lawyer's fees. Hence they remain contained with whatever compensation they got. It was alleged by the people that they got inadequate compensation for their land in compensation to the compensation paid to the neighbouring oustees of NALCO, Angul Sector.

Private property and receiving compensation are inter linked. According to Sing (1989) in relation to land there are two types of citizen in India, those governed by the tendency laws and those governed by the forest laws. Both the groups encroach government land but the former gets the 'Patta' or record of right in due course but the people who belong to the second category never get any record of right because of the enforcement of the forest laws. This is why in almost all the dam projects in India which are located in forest areas have displaced the scheduled caste and tribe people with inferior occupancy right (Sing 1989). There is no security of compensation for them simply because they do not posses any 'Patta' or record of rights for the land even though they are cultivating it from the time to their forefathers.

In a most recent study of seven projects,[7] Pandey has shown that the recipients of compensation in all these seven projects have expressed their discontent regarding the rates fixed by the project authority which they felt, were not par with the prevailing market rates. In fact, the rates determined were actually lower than the replacement value of the acquired assets. It has been alleged that lands were not classified properly and the price of houses and trees were not calculated impartially. The oustees also complained about improper surveys and measurements of houses, wells and ponds by the project authorities (Pandey 1998).

In another survey of 11 projects[8] Fernandes and Raj has studied the land takeover and compensation criteria and they have shown that the majority of displaced persons and project affected persons were not aware of the compensation criteria of the projects authorities and different amount of compensation were paid to different social groups in accordance with their power relation (Fernades and Raj – 1992).

Rao in his Nabakrushna Choudhari Memorial Lecture (1987) had raised an interesting issue of land acquisition by H.S.L. Rourkela as on 1961 H.S.L. at Rourkela has acquired 19, 537.06 acres of land and the amount of land was in excess of the actual requirement of the plant. Since the land so acquired were not put into use the oustees resume unauthorised cultivation on such land (For detail see Rao 1995). Thus the bureaucray acquire land whether that is required or not by showing their bureaucratic power, while the public who are thrown out from their livelihood. Hence there is every reason to suspect the genuineness of the Collector to acquire land for the so called 'Public Purpose'.

According to the L.A. Act 1894 as amended by the state of Orissa the land to be acquired by the Project public or private is to be notified. After the notification the person so affected may file objects to it within thirty days. However one of the study of land acquisition in Dungri Lime Stone Quarry reported that after notification the people were not given time for the petition (Panigrahi and Mishra, nd). In Case of Lanjibrena Lime Stone Quarry when land acquisition took place in 1962 for the construction of staff quarters the notice served in the name of the displaced people weer either pested or hanged on the tree by which the tribals were deprived of knowing and putting up their grivances. After the expiry of the date they were forced either to take low amount of compensation or were left unpaid. (Panigrahi and Mishra, nd). The Lajkura Open Cast Coal Mines of Coal India Limited did not offer any compensation to its oustees for they have no records of right over land. Most of these households were displaced persons from Hirakud Dam Project and it is alleged that they have occupied the land and house-site for which no pattern or record of right can be given to them as such. Hence they were debarred from payment of compensation (Panda and Panigrahi 1987). In one of the M.C.L. Talcher sector land of the village, Jambubahali has been acquired under the L.A. Act 1894 (amended in 1984) for which in Dec 18, 1983. Since the authorities were in a hurry no notification was made under section 5(1) under which the affected person is given a chance to object to land acquisition. The authorities were thus, not given any opportunity to challenge the acquisition of their land (Pandey, 1986).

Saintala Ordnance Industry near Bolangir has acquired 12 thousand acres of land which included 302 acres of land given on lease to more than 150 landless ST and SC households on March 1974. However, at Tahasildar level there was no proper and just records to this effect, hence, Additional District

Magistrate of Bolangir cancelled this lease on February 1989 for which these households were debarred from getting the compensation.

The illustrations can be multiple. For almost in all developmental projects the same 1894 L.A. Act was applied to expropriate the landed property of an individual for public purpose. In all these cases land acquisition was go to legal standing whereas there is no constitutional or legal right of rehabilitation. Hence neither the displacement nor rehabilitation is being done as a matter of right of the people. There is not even any attempts towards a compensatory rehabilitation despite World Bank is insisting on it. The right of the tribals and other usufructiary rights enjoyed by the people in their ancestral lands including the common property resources are not recognised by the state. There is no legal compulsion and Constitutional obligation on the state to rehabilitate the people in order to attain higher quality of life. Compensation is paid on the market value which is a past value and it does not take into consideration the cost escalation or inflationary situation. But what the people require is replacement value than the market value.

Summary and Conclusion

In almost all the projects the Land Acquisition Act 1894 as has been amended in 1984 applied for Land valuation and payment of compensation. Hence Land Acquisition has got legal standing where as there is no constitutional or legal right for rehabilitation. In the absence of a legal compulsion or constitutional obligation on the state to resettle people, rehabilitation has become a bureaucratic charity. The District Collector has been given sample power to decide whether a particular project is for the 'Public Purpose' or not a dictatorial power without any responsibility. Hence there is an urgent need for the amendment of the Land Acquisition Act 1894 to include the following:

(1) Compensation is not given for the common property resources (CRPs). Hence Land Acquisition is to take congnizance of the CRPs.

(2) Compensation is paid on the market values which is a past value and it does not take into consideration the cost escalation on inflationary situation. Hence amendment should include to pay the replacement value than the market values while compensating property.

(3) Enlarge the definition of the project oustees to include married/unmarried sons and daughter of 18 and above age groups, physically and mentally handicapped persons, orphans, divorcees, widows, landless labourers, artisans, village services man, encroacher, grazers, fisherfolk, nomads, forest produce gathers etc.

(4) Full participation of the oustees in the decision concerning the (a) the public purpose of the project, (b) site of the project, (c) magnitude of the impact of the project like displacement environmental pollution, viability of the project cost benefits analysis, rehabilitation of the people etc.

NOTES

1. On March 15, 1946 Sir Willion Harthurun Lewis the then Governor of Orissa, lay the foundation stone of Hirakud Dam Project this was the second time when the construction of the Dam work was inaugurated.
2. Started question no. 11 dated October 11, 1949, Proceeding of the Orissa Legislative Assembly.
3. Stored question no. 690 dated 16-12-1949 Constituent Assembly Proceeding.
4. Orissa Legislative Assembly Proceeding starred questioned no, 1775 dated 25.9.1956.
5. Starred questioned no. 132 dated 8.12.1955 Proceeding of the Orissa Legislative Assembly
6. Harekrushna Mohatab (1964).
7. The projects are (1) Ib Valley Thermal Power Station (ITPS) (2) Ib Valley Coal Mining Projects (MCL) (3) Talcher Coal Mining Project (4) Samal Barrage (5) HAL (6) NALCO Damanjori (7) Upper Kolab Project.
8. The projects are (1) Talcher Super Thermal (2) Talcher Thermal (3) Talchar Fertilizer (4) Talcher Mines (5) NALCO Damanjori (6) NALCO Angul, (7) NALCO Mines Panchapatmali (8) Machkund (9) Upper Kolab (10) Satanding Dam Hudgarh (11) Satkosia Gorge.

REFERENCES

1. Fernandes Walter and S.A. Raj (1992), *Development Displacement and Rehabilitation in the Tribal Areas of Orissa*, Indian Social Institute (ISI) New Delhi.
2. Mahatab Harekrushna (1964), *'Prajatantra'*, Cuttack dtd. 1.1.1964.
3. Nath G.B. (1984), *'Socio-Economic Survey of a Village under Rehabilitation*, ICSSR, New Delhi.
4. Panda, P. and N. Panigrahi (1987): "The Problem of Distacement of Displaced People: A study in the coal mines of Brajraj Nagar," ISSC Seminar Jyoti Bihar, Burla, Samabalpur.
5. Pandey Balaji (1988 a), 'Depriving the underpriviledged for Development', Institute for Socio-Economic Development (TSED) Bhubaneswar.
   (1998 b): Displaced Development: Impact of Open cost mining on Women' ISED, Bhubaneswar.
6. Panigrahi N and A. Mishra (nd) 'In Search of Living: Man and mining in Orissa PRIYA, 45 Soinline from: Khanpur, New Delhi.
7. Rao R.S. (1995): 'Freedom Struggle, Decolonisation and Nabakrushna Choudhary,' In *towards understanding semi Fedual Semi-colonial Society*. Edited by D.N. Reddy perspective, Hyderabad.
8. Sing Chatrapati (1989), 'Rehabilitation and the right to property, in Fernades Thukural (1989) ISI, New Delhi.
9. Ventkat Raman S (1938), *The Land Acquisition Act I of 1894*, Madras Law Journal Press: Madras.

8

Displacement and Deprivation of Tribal People in Orissa

— *Dr. Nilakantha Panigrahi* *

Capitalistic development indeed has widened the informal sector economy and brings a new set of economic and social relationships. One of the important aspects of it is the great expansion of employment. In the process, peasant economy lost commands over material factors for production, which brings them the problem of living. The society becomes weak and gets destabilised since its control over the processes of production is lost due to the impact of many external agencies. Therefore development is intrinsically authoritarian displacing and marginalising the poor and powerless mass on the one hand, and pouring the power of control in hands of bureaucratized elite (Nanda, 1981; Srinivas, 1982; Tripathy, 1988). In such situation the internal solidarity among those who have been displaced by major development projects is no more effective. The holistic character is broken giving rise to major changes in their socio-economic frontiers.

Objectives

With this background the present paper tries to address various issues relating to displacement, and deprivation due to the establishment of development projects in tribal regions of Orissa. Firstly, the paper provides a brief introduction of

---

* *Faculty in Social Anthropology, NKC Centre for Development Studies, Bhubaneshwar (Orissa).*

the problem of displacement, which has oozed out due to development. Secondly, it provides a brief sketch of tribal people of Orissa and their various levels of present development even after five decades of independence. Thirdly, the paper while tracing out the history of displacement (due to development projects established in Orissa), it tries to present the magnitude of the problem, and its impact on tribal people, with special reference to village administration, their economy and family life existed at their native. Fourthly, in the discussion the paper explains certain critical issues observed by World Commission on Dams and tries to, conclude with an anthropological understanding of the problem.

Mega-development projects are the models of economic development recognised across the world. It may be hydro-power project like Sardar Sarovar in Gujarat (the most controversial one in India) and Hirakud Hydro-Power Dam Project constructed in Orissa during 1950s; industrial houses like Rourkela Steel Plant of Orissa or Bhilai Steel Plant in Madhya Pradesh or BHEL in Andhra Pradesh; mining projects in Orissa as well as outside which explores ores like dolomite, iron, bauxite by both Private and Public Sector Companies. All these development projects have immense impact on the physical, social, cultural, psychological life way processes of human societies, in any part of the World, may be in India, Africa or in Argentina; may be in urban or rural areas; may be tribal people and/or non-tribal people. The extent of damage of both natural and man-made resources depends on the size of the project, rate of investment, duration of the construction phase and output as planned. There was a time when these projects were popularly accepted by many world bodies, that such mega-projects are the temples of economic development. Nehru the first Prime Minister of India also called them as 'Temples of modern India'. Perhaps he could not visualize the 'non-economic' threats and effects of such temples, and tried to catch-hold of the religious feelings and emotions of the people. He continued to construct more such temples to see them as the only panacea for economic development and growth. However, experts like Cernea (1987) after five decades found that almost 50 per cent of the World Bank funded projects are not sustainable largely because of their non-institutionalization of peoples' participation.

Magnitude of the Problem

Till date everybody realise that it is very difficult to calculate the magnitude of the problem of displacement in one development project even as a case analysis. The problem not merely includes physical displacement or physical losses (which even difficult to calculate), but also includes the loss of social resources like social integration, community living, culture etc. The loss of these social capital or social resources is unaccountable and not properly taken care even by so called various methods of social-cost-benefit analysis. Quite a couple of studies and reports in various context provide some data on the losses at micro level resulted due to displacement but, the major calculations on the loss of physical resources are popularly provided by few scholars, activists like Cernea, Fernandes, Mathur etc. The figures on human displacement provided by them are both way based on primary as well as secondary estimation of the situation. In Orissan content Mohapatra, Behura, Pande, Stenely, Pattnaik, are few academicians/NGO activists provide an overall understanding on the displacement of manpower due to development projects. The project reports prepared by Government Deptt. only account the figures to whom compensation is paid. The estimations made by the non-Govt. sources is many time criticised by Government due to over estimation, while the non-government agencies and World bodies do not step behind to underestimate the reports prepared by Government authorities, with a plea that Government authorities in such situations always project a lesser extent of loss. The reason for not presenting a proper estimation by both the groups are multiple by nature which have been established over time. So the magnitude of the problem always revolves around the paradigm of over estimation and/or under-estimation, one made by non-Govt. agencies and another made by Govt.

agency. Whatever the extent may be but it is a fact that people lose their life support system in all such cases.

As regards the magnitude of displacement oozing out of these projects there exists a lot of statistical confusions claiming one over another. Cernea one of the expert of World Bank in the context of displacement due to development calculates that involuntary displacement so common now-a-days, and takes place so rampantly that during 20th Century often the figures all over the World goes beyond 10 million every year, of which 6 million are only displaced due to infrastructure development urban sector (1996). However, this do not include the displacement due to the establishment of 'new sectors' like reserve forests, mining and thermal power, and other military test ranges (Cernea 1995). More specifically in Indian context the magnitude of displacement as calculated by Fernandes (2000) for the period 1951-2000 tunes to the extent of 21.3 millions while for academicians like Mohapatra the estimate account this to the tune of 25 millions (1999).

In most of the displacement, which took place due to the establishment of development projects during last couple of decades in various parts of the World in general, and in India and Orissa in particular, it is commonly observed that these projects are largely confined to tribal dominated backward regions. The State imposes and enjoys the right over land, whereas, customarily the local communities i.e. various tribal communities enjoys; the use right over the natural resources for generations together. In order to substantiate the impact of such development projects on the people and the region quite a couple of studies conducted by social geographer or economist (Sawant 1985) or by NGO and social activist, which have basically talked of the provision of infrastructure development and cost benefit analysis, however, the social activist have come forward with their arguments by challenging the very concept of mega-project for the development of people, particularly for the poor. Such a challenge is basically based on the premise that the affected people of a development project belong to one category i.e.

having poor economic base, and due to less or no after care services provided by Government these people suffer a lot in many respect. The invisible losses incurred by these people tempted anthropologists to pock their nose in the matter of displacement issues, which are basically created due to development projects (Scudder, 1973). However, this area was unexpected for the anthropologists in general (Beteille, 1990).

Since 1990 a couple of anthropologists have started their investigation into the issues related to displacement, rehabilitation, resettlement particularly in the context of tribal society (Mohapatra, 1994, 1997, 1998, 1999, 2000; Behura, 1990, 1996; Pattnaik, 1996; Ota, 1996, 1998; Panda and Panigrahi, 1989). They tried to understand the impact of development projects on the socio-cultural life way processes of the oustees in general and tribal people in particular. The common risk factors culminated out of displacement are landlessness, homelessness, joblessnesss, marginalisation, food insecurity, loss of access to common property resources, social disruption and loss of various coping mechanism adopted by the oustees, analysed and discussed by them. Such writings could prove that big dams, minings and other development projects instead of blessing to the people become a boon to the majority of them. They have established that no development will be successful and sustainable if it disrupts the social threads of the society, which dismantles social institutions, social cohesion, and social security system.

The recent years in the field of social research have seen hundreds of research studies on the issue of development and displacement. However, the gamut of anthropological, sociological and social science knowledge of Development. Diplacement and Rehabilitation nexus is yet to be sufficient (Swain and Panigrahi, 1999). Various studies at different point of time highlighted the involuntary displacement at micro level depending on the scholar's biases in favor of people or power. It is no doubt that these studies at micro level help scholars to understand various dimensions of the problem, at the same time enriches the gamut of a social research, but at different point of time these studies in piecemeal are unable to influence the policy-makers to a satisfactory level. This demands an understanding of the problem at macro level so as to influence the policies of the State. In Orissan context a couple of attempts have been made by scholars also to under stand the problem of displacement at macro level.

II

A BRIEF ACCOUNT OF THE TRIBAL SITUATION IN ORISSA

Orissa is located between 17° N to 22.3° Latitudes and between 81.3° to 87.5° E Longitude. It is situated on the Coast of Bay of Bengal, which, is surrounded by Andhra Pradesh on the South. Bay of Bengal on the east, Chhatisgarh on the west and West Bengal and Bihar on the north. The Geo-physical structure of the State is divided into four major zones. Depending upon the agro-climatic features, the state is divided into various productive zones by the Dept. of Agriculture, Govt. of Orissa. These are distributed in various geographical proportions. The State presently covers 1,55,707 sq.km which accounts 4.74 per cent of total land area of the country and geographically ranks in the 9th position among the Indian States. The administrative divisions of the State were formulated with 13 districts during 1948, again restructured into 30 districts in 1992, which are sub-divided into 59 sub-divisons, consisting of 314 Community Development Blocks, comprising of 56,887 number of villages. As regards the population strength is concerned, the State ranks 11th position, and share 3.74 per cent of India's population with a growth rate of 2.00 per cent per annum. Since 1921 the States has experienced a progressive decline in the sex ratio of females. With regards to sex ratio while it was 1086 females per 1000 males in 1921, it has reduced to 927 females during 1991.

Orissa always takes an important, distinct and colorful position in national map by harboring various ethnic groups from the immemorial. Leaving apart the State of Nagaland, the State carries the highest percentage of tribal population in India. Considering the development index, the President of

India during 1956 declared 62 different tribal communities of Orissa as Scheduled Tribes, out of whom 12 no. of communities are considered as Primitive Tribal Group (PTG) for special treatment.

Almost 44.21 per cent of the total land area in Orissa have declared as Scheduled Area. Except the coastal belt, many of the district of the State have been declared either partially or fully as Scheduled Area. The present Scheduled Area of the State covers six districts as fully and seven districts as partially scheduled. The districts of Mayurbhanja, Sundargarh, Koraput, Nawarangpur, Malkangiri and Rayagada are declared as fully Scheduled Areas. Thus, out of 314 Community Development Blocks in Orissa, 118 (37.3%) blocks are preponderantly occupied by the tribal communities which are covered under Tribal Sub-Plan (TSP). The district dominated by tribal communities are Malkangiri (58.74%), Koraput (50.67%), whereas, the district with a sizeable tribal population are Keonjhar (44.62%), Gajapati (47.88%), Jharsuguda (33.88%), Nuapada (35.95%), and Deogarh (33.31%). Thus, the tribal population of Orissa constitute 22.21 per cent of the total State population. The major tribes of Orissa in terms of their numerical strength to name a few are Kondh, Gond, Santal, Saora, Bhuiyan, Paraj, Koya, Oraon, Gadaba, Juanga and Munda. Apart from, there also a good number of smaller tribal communities like Chencu, Juanga, Bonda, Didayi, and Chktia-Bhunjia etc. living in Orissa. Since the latest distribution of population according to different tribewise has not yet been published, here an attempt has been made to look into the census report of 1981 which reflect that the chenchus the smallest tribal community representing only 39 persons. There are 15 tribals group distributed in Orissa, each covering more than on lakh persons. When tribal communities like Santal, Gond, Munda, Ho, Birhor, Koya Lodha, Kondha, Bhumija, Kahra and Oraons cut across the State boundaries and are found in the neighbouring States of Bihar, Chhatisgarh, Andhra Pradesh and West Bengal, the tribal communication like Juanga, Bonda and Didayee are found to be confined to the region of origin in the district of Keonjhar and Malkangirl respectively.

Tribal economy is something more than what economists view in terms of production, distribution and consumption through transaction of goods and services. Therefore, local subsistence economics need to be understood in terms of non-material resources in the context of its culture of the concerned communities. Again an investigation of tribal economy at operational level needs a thorough understanding of the concept o- common property resources which centers around land and forests and the role of encysting non-tribal groups, particularly the Scheduled Castes, like Pano and Doma for mode of use, ownership and control of land. Most of the social scientists have treated land as an object for agriculture and house construction purely from a capitalistic or materialistic viewpoint. However, for the anthropologist land of tribal communities assumes some value beyond a tangible asset. The land is the pivotal property and they attach strong emotions. It has also been found in practice that many tribal communities by and large do not enjoy legal proprietorship over the land they are in occupation for generations. In Orissa the cultivable land came to acquire the status of commodity during British administration. Among tribal communities it could not change the status so easily due to various socio-cultural factors. In tribal societies the practice of corporate and the joint rights over land and land based resources did not allow it to be a salable commodity. For example, the Kutia Kondha and other believe that their ancestors have given land to them and they have no right to sale it.

Forest and forest based resources are inseparable from the life way processes of the tribal people. Unless one goes into the details of worldview of the tribal communities and relates these facts to their native and supernatural entities, the approach to the understanding of tribal societies cannot be a holistic one. Total activities of the tribal communities center on the forest for food, fodder and fuel. The facts of life of the tribal communities thus get entangled to forest. In other words the dependency of the tribal communities on the forest and forest based resources across generations has been guided by their customs and belief pattern. Since forest is an integrated part of tribal communities ultimately they maintain a sympathetic relationship with the forest. The use of various forest produces in the form of leaf, fruits, flowers and other forest bi-products are mainly guided by natural laws, various festive occasions and their traditions. In other words, the functional aspects of the totems and taboos among the tribal communities guide their intimate independence with the nature. The importance of forest resources particularly of the non-timber forest resources has been well ascertained from both the recorded of forest coverage due to various reasons, the dependency of the tribal communities of Orissa on forest and forest based resources since time immemorial, has been very significant till date (Malik and Panigrahi, 1998).

The extent of dependency of the tribal communities on land and forest cannot be clearly understood unless their levels of development is analysed in their ecological context. The shifting agriculture economy a form of subsistence economy, which is still in practice among many north-east and eastern tribal groups. The tribal communities of Orissa like Bhuinya, Juanga, Dangaria Kondh, Kutia, Kondh, Saora, Paraja, Didayi, Koya, Bonda and Gadaba derive their substantial livelihood support from shifting cultivation. Compared to many other parts of India the India the extent of practicing shifting cultivation is no way less significant among the tribes of Orissa. In spite of the changes in the practise of shifting cultivation due to various reasons like development intervention, population growth and imposition of legal ownership for individual holdings its effects are still felt by all sections of the society (Mallik, *et al.* 1998). Shifting cultivation is still practiced in diminished magnitude for the that it is intimately associated with the way of life among the isolated small communities inhabiting in the hills and plateaus of Orissa.

The tribal communities of Orissa seem to have shown remarkable performance in managing their land and land-based resources (O.R.G. 1985; Kant *et al.* 1991; Jonson and Rabi, 1994; Saxena, 1995). Above all, it is a fact that forest of Orissa has always got a recognized place in term of providing precious resources to both its dwellers and State Exchequer.

For example timber and bamboo are the major forest produces, constituting 76.0, 87.0 and 75.0 per cent of the total forest revenue of our State earned during 1991-92, 1992-93 and 1995-96 respectively (Govt. of Orissa, 1996-97).

III
DISPLACEMENT IN ORISSA

The adoption of planned development in the form of Five Year Plans since 1952 in India basically aims to minimise the poverty. Most of the mega-projects are located in resourceful regions which are by and large inaccessible. Due to variations in the socio-cultural bases, so the impact of these projects on the people and the area are also differential. At certain level these projects have up-heaveled the age-old harmony between settled population and their environment (Behura, 1996). A few of such mega-projects so far we have in Orissa when classified reflects that among Multi-Purpose Hydro-Electric Projects which involved large scale displacement of people and caused disruption of bio-physical and socio-cultural resources are: Machakund (1949), Hirakud (1948), Balimela (1963), Rengali (1973), Upper Kolab (1978), Upper Indravati (1978), while the industrial and Mining Projects which are also caused similar impact in Orissa are: Hindustan Aeronautic Limited in Koraput (1962), Bauxite Mining in Koraput (1981) and Sambalpur (1988), Allumina Smelter Plant at Angul (1985), Steel Plant at Gopalpur (in process) (1996), and many more mining projects in the districts of Sundargarh, Keonjhar, and Mayurbhanja operating since 1940. A cursory estimate made by Frenandes and ASIF (1995) on the displacement of human population in Orissa due to the establishment of these mega-projects from 1951 to 1995 clearly reflects that Hydro-Electric Multi-Purpose Projects have displaced 3,25,000 people of which only 90,000 people (27.69%) have been rehabilitated. Similarly, due to industrial projects out of 71,794 displaced people in Orissa only 27,300 (30.03%) have been rehabilitated; while mining projects displaced around 1,00,000 people of which almost 60.00 per cent people have been rehabilitated; and due to declaration of sanctuary around 50,000 people have been displaced of which only 15,540 (31.08%) are rehabilitated. In total these mega-projects under the agies of planned development during a period of four and half decades have displaced around 5,46,794 people of which only 35.27 per cent (1,92,840) people have been rehabilitated.

From another calculation it is put forth by the scholars that of the total oustees in India around 50.00 per cent are belonging to different tribal communities and other weaker sections (Fernandes, 1991). Similarly, in India from 1951 to 1976 due to planned development in the field of agriculture, industries, water control projects, construction of roads and railways and raising of planned settlements, approximately 4136 thousand hectares of forest vegetation have been cleared, and during last two decades i.e. from 1976 to 1996 another 2500 hectares of forest land are believed to have been uprooted for various development purpose (Behura, Ibid).

Here specific attempt has been made to estimate the displacement made due to the construction of few hydro-electric projects in backward inland region of Orissa. The data (Table 1) reflects that during the period of 1949 to 1978 six number of such projects have been constructed which has affected 1112 villages, and submerged an area of 4,14,615 acres. These projects have displaced 56, 325 no. of families which has affected 3,15,801 no. of people, of which only 13,228 no. of families have been rehabilitated. Similarly taking six industrial and mining projects constructed during the period of 1962 to 198 in Orissa (Table 2) an analysis has been made which reflects that 42,370 acres of land have been acquired in 116 no. of villages which has displaced 8763 no. of families affecting 44442 people.

Impact of Displacement on Tribal People

Impact of displacement can be seen in various fronts of human society. Displacement may affect the bio-physical resources, livelihood-resources of both human society as well as at destination. While highlighting four major hydro-electric project, industrial and mining projects of Orissa Swain and

Panigrahi (1999) in their paper tried to visualize all oozed out problems through five categories. They are viz. loss of property and compensation, process of displacement and people's reaction , resettlement and rehabilitation. Similarly, Panda and Panigrahi (1986) while studying the problems of double displacement one due to the construction of Hirakud Dam Project and secondly, due to coal mining operations in Brajrajnagar highlighted the socio-economic and socio-cultural dimensions of displacement. Behura (1996) while studying the Rengali oustees has also highlighted the importance of social institutions, which act as social threads and maintain the social solidarity of the rural people and its losses due to such displacement. This section tries to find out the impact of displacement in the tribal society of Orissa specifically with respect to village power structure, village economy and family life existed in their traditional villages. The description apparently seems to be a romanticisation of the past. However, a loss is a loss. For the loss of material goods some amount of quantification is possible, but for the loss in socio-cultural and psychological frontiers it is not an easy task. The loss incurred can hardly be viewed as something romanticisation.

Impact on Village Economy

Forest produces contribute a lot in the tribal economy. The tribal people at their native were collecting leafy vegetables, fruit and roots, which supports their livelihood sustenance. Occasionally the tribal people were also getting forest games mostly consumed by them and the fortunate used to collect honey, which are consumed and sold in the market. Apart from supplying food, fodder, and fuel the forest at their native was also supping medicines to the inhabitants. In a sense prior to displacement forest was a major source of living for these people. In this way the villages mostly dominated by tribal people in these backward regions were self-sufficient with their land and forest resources.

With the technical knowledge and the available natural resources, in predisplacement situations at native villages each family was acting as an unit of production. Since the field of their work was around the house, the house, the housewives along with their all-household works were also able to share the workload of their male folks. The villages were functioning either on the basis of *'Jajmani system'* or *'panchas'* in caste and tribal dominated villages respectively. Each family was running with certain rights and duties in relation to its caste families and village structure. Even though child labour was not recognised in the village till the parents honoured casual labour of the children in the family. So the members of the family honored each other's contribution.

The simple living standard and the fulfillment of minimum needs coupled with prescribed status were almost creating no internal conflicting groups within the village. The village ceremonies and festivities were the areas to minimise the tensions if such cases appear among them. However, it varies from a tribal village to multi-caste village. The holistic character of the villages were reflected in their customs and traditions through communal rituals, and group sharing of liquor, communal dance, village fare, and festivals. These were providing them a sense of fraternal feeling. Besides this, in multi-caste village the *'Bhagabat Tungi'* was playing an important role for the maintenance of village solidarity. It was a place where members of different caste sit together and listen to the *abdhan* or the village heads. The adherence of these social rules and practice of traditional songs, riddles, folk dances and fear of village rumor were important events to maintain social distance and social control among the boys and the girls of married and unmarried groups. In multi-ethnic villages even though the caste people were economically well off and were of numerically stronger, the representation of the minority groups in village decision in process was accommodated for socio-economic protections. So, people of different origins were not only sharing the pleasure but also taking interest in renovating and cleaning ponds, decorating dance arena, purifying shrines etc. In other one can say that the homogeneity and homogenous feeling within the heterogeneity coupled with mutual honour of their religion and traditions were the major cause for their dynamic social solidarity. In this regard Pathy writes that 'they were leading a life of primordial and religious ties rooted in history, polity, and in social structure (1987).

Impact of Family Life

Family as an institution plays a vital role in the life way processes of the people. The control over the processes of production from agriculture, forestry and manual skill such as blacksmithy, carpentry, pottery, cow herding, washing clothes practised at native have been ceased at destination. So this abrogation of household crafts based on traditional knowledge and the resulted technological gap forced the housewives to remain inside the house. Even the children who were contributing their labour as desired by families could not get scope to enhance the traditional skill and knowledge. More especially this was the case with fisherman, cobbler, and jhara caste families and with many tribal communities in the displaced regions of the State. So the displacement of housewives and children from the productive process forced them to depend on the household head, which some time led to more male superordination within the family. In this process the family turned from a unit of independent productive center to a dependent group on male casual labourer. Late, due to economic compulsion the wives and children started working outside as casual labourer. This gave way to the breakage of earlier family bond, which in subsequent periods encouraged liquor habit, prostitution and juvenile delinquency among the oustees.

Along with other customary element, the liquor has a significant role in the social life of the tribal people. To meet the cultural necessities it was prepared by them through various indigenous methods. But now the availability of liquor from shops and depose tempted them, and many of them have started purchasing from the vendor. For the vendors to dupe them in this process became an easy task. The illiterate displaced tribal people mostly did not know the use value of money. Taking the advantage of their cultural necessities the liquor vendors exploited then through various means. The group sharing of liquor in festive occasions and also during evening hour where normally they used to ventilate their pains and share pleasure no more existed. The ready availability of liquor made the evening gossip groups casual, and changed the contents. The inter-personal relationship, which was once, based on kinship and lineage/clan is destroyed and become unimportant. The village elders normally who were related each other through their kin bond or otherwise could get no scope to maintain in harmony. Due to the displacement, members of lineage/clan dispersed in search of employment, as a result, social groups are formed having no mutuality and cultural base. Thus, it made their attitude indifferent towards each other in their social behavior and reflected the sudden abrogation of community life. The existing infrastructure does not accommodate them as per their cultural needs, and exposed them to an alien culture. So the large scale eviction, the loss of their lands, destruction of their places of worship and burial grounds disoriented them culturally and weakened their collective solidarity, made them vulnerable to the blandishment of the government in terms of cash compensation (Ghosh, 1987).

The impact of movies, T.V. obscene picture, cinema songs, modern dresses is another arena, which have generated empathy towards their traditional songs, dances, and ornaments. The youth dormitories, village *kothaghar* named differently among different tribal communities no more remained as a source of renewing their moral and religious sanctions. The impersonal social gatherings are observed at liquor depose or at the tea stall. Gambling and cinema replace the traditional forms of recreation. This took them far away from their own traditions and customs. The community festivals, which were earlier very important for building their social organisations and for maintaining for social cohesion, have been broken down. The social distance maintained by boys and girls, married and unmarried has undergone changes. Among tribal people the inter-ethnic marriages were unthinkable in earlier days. However, now cases of inter-ethnic marriages have been reported. The term *'budi anchalar lok'* and/or homeless have been affecting them as a social stigma in their matrimonial relations. The kith and kin that have exchanging their daughter in marriages among themselves were ceased to continue. The primary reasons for not giving daughters in marriage to the people of these household is that they will have no security, because there exists no lineage and clan, no land, and no forest for these groups. Perhaps this is the reason for which the elopement is frequent among the displaced tribal people. Even due to the social dis-organisation the daughters of the poor displaced families have to share beds of the haves for their livelihood (observed in urban areas). This has also given way to the poor girls to get into prostitution. Displacement not only put them in problems in social, economic, cultural and psychological spheres, but also brought about ecological hazard due to mining projects and industrial development (Panda and Panigrahi, 1987).

Impact on Village Power Structure

The power structure in a tribal village includes the administrative head, religious head and the messenger. People performing these specific functional roles are known in different names in different tribal communities. Since tribal villages are integrated territorial units so these people enjoy region specific roles. It is believed that these traditional leaders were also enjoying supernatural blessings for their action and decisions.

For generation together tribal villages are run/managed by a system of traditional authority structure purely internal to the community. Such a structure exercise various powers with respect to the economy of the villages: by distributing shifting land patches, controlling the in-out-migration, and maintaining an harmonic relation within the villages; socio-cultural lives of the villagers: by deciding the punishment for social deviants, giving justice through village panchayats, maintaining social disciplines by enjoying control over the people etc. It is reported that in earlier situations the village conflicts were resolved within the village. The internal differentiation was not very much sharp. There was almost no conflicting groups, might be due to the dominance of *Gountias* and *Naiks*. The village heads that remained as landlord of the village with respect to *royats* and to the representatives of the Government for collection of revenue and in the management of village affairs was assigned with village administration.

In case of displacement situations so far experienced due to mega-projects in Orissa the data shows that the rehabilitation and resettlement of these people (oustees) many time goes beyond the managerial and resource capacity of the Government. As a result, in all cases the oustees are involuntary and forceful without having any planned arrangements for all. In such cases the tribals villages as territorial entity losses their control over people and disgracefully dismantled resulting out migration. If a group of tribal people are settled in few colonies as happened in many displaced situations in Orissa there arises a new type of leadership being encouraged by both Government functionaries as well as non-tribal people. As a result, the traditional authority structures in new situations are unable to cope with the emerging agents both within and outside. The introduction of Panchayati Raj system in newly established tribal villages the Government functionaries did not tried to cope with the old leadership pattern on the premise that the new democratic principles do not believe on the importance of traditional leadership structure. The new democratic authorities could not visualize and understood the importance of traditional political structures, which has played a dynamic role in the internal administration of tribal societies.

IV

DISCUSSION

During 1990 there was a strong debate between the supporter and the critics of large dams, which later on forced the World Bank to withdraw the financial support from few large dam projects including the Sardar Sarovar Project in India. The Dams and development report of World

Commission on Dams (thus known as WCD) released during November 2000 again highlights debates on the impact of such dams on the environment and socio-cultural life of the people. The forces behind forming such a commission to study dams originated from the congregation of 800 Government, NGOs, dam builders, equipment supplier, human right groups who met at Switzerland during April 1997 to find out key issues relating to the social, environmental, technical and financial aspects of dams. The task given to WCD was firstly to review the development effectiveness of large dams and asses alternatives for water resources and energy development; and secondly, to develop internally acceptable criterias, guidelines and standards which will be appropriate for the planning, design appraisal, construction, operation, monitoring and decommissioning of the dams. The International Commission on Large Dams (ICOLD) a body of engineer with 80 national committees; the International Commission on Irrigation and Drainage (ICID) which too had 94 national committees; Project Evaluation Report of World Bank etc. had also arrived at conclusions with regards to the debate on dam-development and people. They have highlighted the effects of large dams on the environment, society, culture and social, environment of the people.

The WCD report has tried to highlight the areas to improve the planning and decision-making processes for such big dams while adopted in the future, and emphasized various lessons experienced in the yester years. They highlighted the "right to risk" approach than merely talking old-style-cost-benefit analysis. Reacting to the WCD report the Ministry of Water Resources of Government of India commented that WCD report gives certain disturbing observations with respect to equity, alternatives and options, consultation and participation. It commented that the concept of stakeholders which is ethically neutral a flawed one which has potential for misuse by saying that all politicians, bureaucrats, engineers, consultants and contractors are all stakeholder standing on one footing with differential interest and concern. By treating everybody as stakeholder the focus on the affected people (who are also treated equally as stakeholders) and their specialty has been questioned.

Table 1

Notable Multipurpose Hydro-electric Projects in Orissa involving Large Scale Displacem ent

Projects	Year of Estb.	Submerged (Nos.) Village	Area Acres	Family	People	Rehabilitation Families (Nos.)
1	2	3	4	5	6	7
Machakund	1949	225	20,794	2,938	14,690	600
Hirakud	1948	285	1,82,593	22,144	1,60,000	1,879
Balimela	1963	89	48,000	2,000	9,600	NA
Rengali	1973	265	1,05,905	10,847	54,235	6,639
Upper Kolab	1978	149	24,794	13,095	50,771	525
Upper Indravati	1978	99	32,530	5,301	26,505	9,585
Total		1112	4,14,615	56,325	3,15,801	13,228

Source: Various Published Sources

However, certain basic questions are coming to our mind that whether dams and mega-projects are acceptable or not acceptable to the human society? In spite of qualitative changes in the planning, monitoring and evaluation processes adopted to have such mega-projects during last couple of years, is it desirable to have big dams for environment and to the society at large. The rationality behind pro-dam and anti-dam movement is still a big question before the human society. The experience shows that weather the expected benefits of a mega-project (may it mineral, industrial, and/or water based) is achieved as it was planned both in terms of output and target period for service delivery? Weather these projects are cost effective, if at all, what are the sacrifices the society has made? Weather social cost–benefit analysis of these mega-projects are made properly during projects formulation stage or it was under-estimated and/or over estimated and these became jargons made by the experts to justify the projects more theoretically than practically. In case of mega-projects what ever benefits have been so far accrued for the people at the cost of various resources weather any alternatives are thought or not?

The nature, method and approach for an empirical study largely depends on the scholar's background. Among the social scientists anthropologists maintain their social distinct due to the methodologies they adapt to study a community and their problems. The community approach of understanding social problems by and large lacking in other disciplines (partly except sociology and social work). Since the gamut of social research in respect of the problem of displacement which takes place due to mega-projects in early days was mainly carried out by non-anthropologists, so these studies have contributed a lot in shaping the study findings various approach. However, with the entry of anthropologists who consider social problems as a part of larger social system tried to understand displacement not merely as a physical movement of people, but also a movement of social institutions. Due to their nature of study anthropologists particularly social-anthropologists highlighted the importance of and the influence of displacement over social institution, social practices, ethnic relation through emic-approach both at native as well as destination. Adoption of kinship studies through genealogy, case studies, longitudinal and diachronically perspective on the social life of the displaced people and the affected universe has made anthropological studies distinct, which are new in the history of displacement studies. In later period new dimension and techniques have been adopted to study livelihood issues, social adaptation, and identity crisis of the oustees when they are either settled in a new eco-system and/ or left open to leave to go as they like. Infusing such dimensions in the study of displacement in later period anthropologists have contributed a lot for other scholars to understand the importance of pri-mordial character in the life and livelihood of the displaced. The temporal model of resettlement phases (Scudder, 1993) and the impoverish model

(Cernea, 1993) has influenced anthropologists so also influenced by anthropological understanding of the existence of a symbiotic relationship among people, habitat and displacement. All these analysis favoured and rationalized the need of mega-projects as the only solution for peoples development. But the paradigm still prevails that the quality of human life is largely depends on the type of development approaches "quantitative and/or qualitative" adopted by State.

Table 2

Displacement in Few Industry and Mining Projects in Orissa

Project	Year	Land Acquired (Ac.)	No. of Villages	No. of Families Displaced	Total Population
1	2	3	4	5	6
Hindustan Aeronautic Ltd. in Koraput	1962	7,200	10	1,200	6,000
Bauxite Mining in Koraput	1981	5,936	41	788	3,104
Bauxite Mining in Sambalpur	1985	2,379	24	1,396	9,111
Steel Plant at Rourkela in Sundargarh	1962	19,557	30	2,467	12,335
Steel Plant at Gopalpur in Ganjam	1996	7,598	11	2,912	13,892
Alluminium Smelter Plant at Angul	1985	3,828	3	Nil	Nil
Total		42,370	116	8,763	44,442

Source: Various Published Sources.

Table 3
Distribution of Displaced due to Various Projects and their Rehabilitation in Orissa from 1951 to 1995

Type of Projects	Total Displaced	D.P. Rehabilitated	% of Rehabilitation	D.P. Not Rehabilitated	% of Not Rehabilitation
1	2	3	4	5	6
Hydro-Electric Multi-Purpose	3,25,000	90,000	27.69	2.35,000	72.31
Industrial	71,794	27,300	38.03	44,494	61.97
Mining	1,00,000	60,000	60.00	40,000	40.00
Others (Sanctuary etc.)	50,000	15,540	31.08	34,460	68.92
G. Total	5,46,794	1,92,840	35.27	3,53,954	64.73

Source: Fernandes & Asif: 1995

REFERENCES

1. Acharya, P. K. Mishra, R. Panigrahi, N. and R. P. Mohanty (2001), Functioning of Welfare Schemes for the Scheduled Castes and Scheduled Tribes: A Report on Orissa, Submitted to the Committee of Governors of India. NKC Centre for Development Studies, Bhubaneshwar.
2. Behura, N. K. (1990): Socio-Economic problems and Social Change. In : *The Uprooted*, (ed). V. Sundersen and M. A. Kalam, New Delhi: Gian Publishing House.
3. --------- (1996), Environment, Displacement and Development: Case Study from Orissa, *Journal of Indian Anthropology Society*, 31:149-159.
4. Behura, N. K and Nayak, P. K. (1193): Involuntary Displacement and the Changing Frontiers of Kinship: A study of Settlement in Orissa. In *Anthropological Approaches to Resettlement*, (ed). Michael M. Crenea and Scot E. Guggenheim.
5. Crenea, M.M (1995), Understanding and Preventing Impoverishment from Displacement: Reflections on the State of Knowledge. Keynote address at International Conference on Development Induced Displacement and Impoverishment, Oxford University.
6. -------- (1996), "Risks and Reconstruction Model for Resettling Displaced Population", *EPW*, June 15.
7. Fernades, W. (1994), *Development induced Displacement in the Tribal Areas of Eastern India*, New Delhi: Indian Social Institute (Mimeo).
8. Iyer, R. R. (2001), "World Commission of Dams and India: Analysis of a Relationship", *EPW*, Vol. XXXVI, No. 25, pp. 2275-2281.

9. Mohapatra, L. K. (1998), Participatory Approach in Resettlement and Rehabilitation Implementation, Paper presented at Gopabandhu Academy of Administration, in the Seminar on Resettlement and Rehabilitation.
10. -------- (1999), *Resettlement, Impoverishment and Reconstruction in India: Development for the Deprived.* New Delhi: Vikash Publishing House.
11. -------- (1999a), Testing the Risks and Reconstruction Model: The Socio-Economics of Poverty in India's Resettlement Practice. In M .M. Cernea (ed) *The Economics of Involuntary Resettlement: Questions and Challenges,* Washington D.C. The World Bank.
12. Navalawala, B. N. (2001), "World Commission on Dams: Biased?", *EPW,* Vol. XXXVI. No. 2, pp. 1008-1010.
13. Ota, A.B. (1998), Countering Impoverishment Risks: The Case of Rengali Dam Projects. In: H.M. Mathur and David Marsden (ed) *Development Projects and Impoverishment Risks.* Delhi: Oxford University Press.
14. Pande, B. *et al.* (1998): Depriving the Underprivileged for Development. Institute for Socio-Economic Development, Bhubaneswar.
15. Panda, P and Panigrahi, N. (1989): The Problem of Displaced People: A study in the Coal Mines of Brajraj Nagar, Sambalpur Orissa. (ed) Tribal Development in India R.N. Pati and B. Jena. Ashish Publication House.
16. Patnaik, S.M. (1996), *Displacement, Rehabilitation and Social Change,* New Delhi: Inter-India Publications.
17. -------- (2000), "Understanding Involuntary Resettlement: An Anthropological Perspective". *The Eastern Anthropologist.* Vol. 53, Nos. 1-2, Jan-June 2000.
18. Pathy, J.(1987), *Ethnic Minorities and Processes of their Development,* UGC Report.
19. Swain, M and Panigrahi, N. (1999), "Development, Displacement and Rehabilitation in Orissa: An Overview", *Man and Life.* Vol. 25, Nos. 3 and 4, July-Dec.

9

Rehabilitation and Development for Hirakud Oustees

— *Dr. Chitrasen Pasayat**

Very recently the Chief Minister (CM) of Orissa on one fine Friday morning has expressed his deep concern over the fact that problems of the inhabitants, displaced by Hirakud dam about fifty years ago, are yet to be settled. He has directed his officials to regularise the Pattas/Record of Rights (RORs) of land given to the oustees in a fixed time frame. During his visit to Samabalpur on August 17, 2001, the CM has chaired a meeting on problems of people displaced by Hirakud Dam Project. The RDC (North) has assured the CM that all the RORs will be regularised by December 30, 2001 and the compensation amounts will also be disbursed by then.[1] This is neither a new nor a good news: because during past fifty years governments have come and gone and they have repeatedly made such commitments and assurances but failed to solve the problems of Hirakud oustees. The present paper is primarily based on inspiration of three noble hearts, who have experienced and shared a lot of pains with these displaced persons. All of them have already left this mortal earth for good. One of them was Sri Purandar Pasayat, father of the author and the other two were Sri Prasanna Panda and Sri Sraddhakar Supakar, an academician and formerly Members

* *Dr. Pasayat, O.A.S., Assistant Administrator, Jagannath Temple, Puri (Orissa).*

of Legislative Assembly (MLA) in Orissa. Informations contained in this paper were provided mainly by these noble souls.

Pandit Jawaharlal Nehru, the first Prime Minister (PM) of independent India laid the foundation stone of the main Hirakud dam on April 13, 1948. Reportedly, both the state as well as the Central Government promised land for land, house for house and adequate compensation to the people of this area that submerged under the project. This was, perhaps, the first Mega project of its kind started in Orissa after Independence. But the idea was conceived and given a beginning earlier during the British Raj. It is attested by the fact that earlier on March 15, 1946, Sir Hawthorne Lewis, the then Governor of Orissa first laid the foundation stone of this project. Speaking on the occasion, Mr. H.C. Prior, the Secretary to Governor of India, said on behalf of the Government of India regarding the resettlement and compensation payable to the persons to be displaced from the Hirakud submerged area. The question of compensation and resettlement "will need careful and sympathetic handling but the Scheme will have such vast potentiality that it is hoped that it will be found possible to find compensation in the form of land in villages properly designed to combine the benefits of agriculture and industry".[2]

As per the Hirakud Dam Project Report, "The Policy of the Government should be to give, as far as possible, land in exchange for land and that well ahead of actual submergence. The compensation in kind or cash should be on terms which are equitable and if anything generous. Government should assist the people in rehabilitation and strive to create conditions in the new colonies, which should be a definite improvement on existing ones. This can be done by setting up model villages and providing them with essential amenities like drinking water, sanitation, public schools, community centres, electricity etc. Any expenditure on such improvements, which is in excess of the compensation allowance in the project should be met from the general revenue as a contribution towards raising the standard of living of the people".[3] While speaking on the benefits of this project, on September 5, 1946, the CM made his observations on the floor of Assembly, "Against forty or fifty thousands acres of Agricultural land submerged, some eight hundred thousand acres will be brought under irrigation, a great part of which will be new cultivation so that the output of rice should increase many times".[4] He further stated, "Supposing now the Government proceeds to provide land to the landless people, there in Sambalpur and elsewhere by clearing jungle and wasteland, it must go the credit of any Government. With regard to the remaining percentage of the population, as I have already mentioned, I promise that more than ample compensation will be given to them for the loss which they might sustain."[5]

As per the instructions of the Director of Public Relations, Government of Orissa, the District Public Relation Officer (DPRO), Sambalpur carried on extensive propaganda in the district that land for land and house for house would be provided to the displaced persons.[6]

According to pamphlets with attractive picture coverage of houses, water taps, roads and machines including other big promises were sold as golden dreams to the people free of cost. In the mean time, the Orissa Government introduced the legislation in the State Assembly without further loss of time. For some, this was a diabolical legislation and a measure adopted by the State government to deprive the people of their legitimate dues, who were to be displaced from the project area. All the same, this Act 18 of 1948 as characterised by some critics left the displaced persons at the mercy of the Special Land Acquisition Officer. As per the provisions laid down in this Act, appeal against the decision of LAO was to be heard by an Arbitrator appointed for the project." The result was devastating and the Act ruined the lives of thousands of displaced person. A few illustrations rations from the proceedings of the State Legislative Assembly subscribe this truth. In order to construct the workshop Ac. 27.26 decimals of land were acquired from 24 families in Jamda village.[7] Possession of land was taken on April 2, 1948 and after one year, payment of compensation was started on April 14, 1949.

The total amount of compensation was Rs. 519.50 only for 27 acres and 76 decimals of land. In other words, a little more than eighteen rupees per acre was determined towards compensation to these people. Most of the recipients of compensation were Scheduled Castes (SCs), Scheduled Tribes (STs) and widows. It would not be out of context to mention here that the foundation stone of the project was laid in March, 1946, but the first reclamation centre was inaugurated almost after three years on February 13, 1949. "This was a clear indication of lack of sincerity of the government about the problem of rehabilitation of the Hirakud oustees"—said one victim of this mega project.

No one was really happy with this meagre amount of compensation to the displaced families of Jamda village. There was uproar in the State Assembly. Sri Dinabandhu Sahu, one Senior MLA asked, "So the government accept the implication of the question that the rate of compensation is too law?" CM replied "Low or not, Payment has been made according to the agreement between the ryots and the government." There was another supplementary question, "Has compensation been paid at the rate of three annas per decimal land ?" CM Replied "What is objectionable there? If ryots accept compensation at three annas per decimal, what is the objection?"

It may be pointed out here that these 24 families were deprived of their lands, hearths and homes in April 1948 and not a single anna was paid to them for more than one year, deserting them homeless, landless and penniless. On another occasion CM said,"As I have already said the compensation is paid with the agreement of the parties. If the parties did not agree, it was open to them to come to the court". The CM further stated that the compensation paid to them was much more than the ordinary rates provided in the law.[8] The following analysis would subscribe the fact that compensation amount was not at all adequate and equitable.

Everybody has always reiterated that the compensation has been awarded for the benefits of the displaced persons. On August 5, 1950, Sri Sadasiv Tripathy, Revenue Minister of Orissa also observed the same thing, "I want to make it clear that under the order of the Central Government, the compensation that we have give to our brothers is to benefit them." Apparently, it became a mere political statement having no intrinsic values. Thousands were driven from their homes and land without payment of a single anna. Government did not pay any attention and examine the rate and amount of compensation given to the Hirakud oustees as compared to others i.e. other than people from the Hirakud submerged area. There was absolutely no equitable distribution of compensation, even the rate of compensation varied from place to place. It is attested from the following example. The Government of Orissa acquired land in the village Barapli (in present Bargarh district and is situated about sixty Kms away from the submerged area) for a High School and Government farm. The total amount of compensation paid for Ac. 116.85 decimals of land was Rs. 98,589 and three annas. This may be worked out at a little less than Rs. 850 per acre and this rate was nearly 47 times more than that of compensation to the Jamda villagers, who were mostly poor SCs, STs and widows. This compensation was paid in 1948 and 1949.[9] In the year 1947, the Government acquired Ac. 23.9 decimals of land in the village Telenpali which was very close to the reservoir area and a sum of Rs. 23,586 was awarded to the people. This may be worked out a little less than Rs. 983 per acre. Undoubtedly, this rate of compensation was more than fifty times the rate paid to the displaced people of Jamda. What we want to point out here is that, the rate of compensation was never maintained uniformly by the State Government. The rate was something for the Hirakud oustees and something for others. It is also true to note here that the Hirakud oustees never received much more than the ordinary rate prescribe in the law as claimed by the Government from time to time.

It was really a difficult task to estimate the number of persons exactly driven out of their houses without payment of compensation. Most probably, the number was estimated to be around fifty thousand. Reportedly, the CM had once stated in the floor of Assembly that three annas per decimal was more than the legitimate dues of compensation for the people displaced from the Hirakud submerged area. In an article in the Oriya daily The Prajatantra (published from Cuttack), dated January 1, 1964, the editor[10] wrote that the real cultivators were in great distress for not getting proper compensation. He regretted that though compensation began to be paid ten to twelve years earlier, the work had not been completed. In fact this was the irony. Notably, the editor of the Prajatantra was Sri Harekrushna Mahatab, who was the CM of the State for twice, first from 1945 to 1952 and then from 1957 to 1961. It was during his time that the idea of the Hirakud Dam Project was conceived and given a shape. Practically speaking there was no common justice for the Hirakud oustees. The person who could raise voice against the injustice and discrimination by the Government, he could manage to get specific justice. The following example will substantiate the above fact. There was a landlord who challenged the arbitrary award of the compensation. Subsequently, the matter went up to the Orissa High Court which approved for higher compensation. Orissa High Court which approved payment of compensation at a rate which was sixteen times the net produce of the land. This came to around Rs. 750 per acre, which was forty times more than the rate at which the ryots were being paid by the government. As per the order of the court, the Government was obliged to pay compensation for the landlord's land at that rate.[11] It was the time when a socialist congressman namely Nabakrushna Choudhury was the CM of Orissa (from 1952 to 1957). For some people of Sambalpur, he could have easily made appropriate changes in 1948 Act in order to bring the rate at which the ryots were being paid compensation at par with the High Court order. Undoubtedly, the landlord class of this area could exert pressure for a higher rate of compensation for their lands than they deserved.

As per the 1948 Act, the person who was claiming compensation at a rate higher than the rate offered by the Hirakud Land Acquisition Officer, he had to reply to the notice of the offer of the compensation within seven days of the receipt of such notice. But there was no limit of the interval of time between the date of reply and the date when the cases should be referred to the Arbitrator. Allegedly, the Government restored to the method of arm-twisting by suppressing such applications for years together. For instance, notices were given in 1955 summer to the residents of fifty villages in the submerged area to vacate their lands and homes. It would not be out of context to mention here that most of these villagers had applied since 1951, at least to send their cases to the Arbitrator for determination of proper compensation. But, these applications were suppressed for four long years. Thus the officials were allegedly on the look out for new methods of harassing the submerged area people. Fifty-seven villages were evacuated in the summer of 1955, and the whole area of 288 square miles was evacuated by July, 1956, when the reservoir was first filled with water. Thousands of families who were promised land for land house for house were immediately forced out of their lands and houses with the help of police like dumb and driven cattle without payment even a single anna. The strength of Police force deputed in April and May, 1955 for the purpose of evacuation was seven Sub-Inspectors, five Havildars and 52 Constables. In addition to this, every day fifty Constables were detailed with trucks carrying the displaced persons. Three platoons of Orissa Military Police (OPM) and eleven Battalion Dhenkanal were also deputed, out of which there NCDS and eighteen sepoys were deputed to three interior camps each under the control of a Magistrate to maintain law and order. The remaining OMP personnel were kept as stand by in the Police line, Sambalpur.[12]

Two hundred villages were likely to be submerged partly or fully during the monsoon of 1956. Notices under Rule 4 of the Special Land Acquisition Act, 1948 were issued in one hundred villages and notices were still to be issued in the remaining villages by 8th December, 1955.[13] Notably, Rule 4 notice was preliminary notice which provided that at least one year interval was necessary for the issue of such notice and payment of compensation. The callousness of the Officials may be attested further by the following facts. The statistics of about 15000 families likely to be evacuated from the area during the monsoon of 1956 were collected and 7547 families were paid compensation in full as per the claim made by the State Government.[14]

But when asked on the floor of the Assembly, the CM had no specific information on how much compensation was exactly paid to these families. "Time and tide waits for none; the reservoir was filled up in July-August, 1956 and the Hirakud Oustees looked at one another in dismay"– was the agony expressed by one Hirakud oustee. Even after the submergence, the law was flouted in order to deprive the Hirakud oustees of their legitimate dues. This may be substantiated by the following facts. Reportedly, 2540 cases in which objections under Rule 5 were filled, were not referred to the Arbitrator by the Hirkud land Organisation till September 25, 1956.[15]

Nearly 4000 families were evacuated in 1955 and 10,352 families were evacuated in 1956 from the submerged area under the Hirakud Dam, and the amount of compensation payable to them was estimated to be Rs. 4,67,94,937 only. Out of these 14,352 families, only 3098 were not paid compensation in full.[16] Significantly, as per the Khosla Report, the total cost of land acquisition was roughly estimated to be Rs. 5,68,62,635 only. In other words, the State Government made a net saving of nearly one crore of rupees or about twenty percent by under–paying or postponing payment of compensation. "How generous the government" was the fact. Once Sri Prasanna Panda recalled that thirty two years after the Hirakud reservoir was filled up a question was put in 1988 on the floor of the Assembly. CM answered that in 5913 cases of the lands acquired from the Hirakud oustees, a sum of Rs. 15,41,469=94 paise only remained unpaid because the oustees did not turn up to take their compensation money and as a result the money was kept as revenue deposit in Sambalpur. This answer was a cruel joke–said Panda. Almost all of the 9913 claimants might have run to the Special Land Acquisition Officer again and again with a hope to fetch their dues. They probably expected to be paid at a rate higher than that of eighteen rupees and twelve annas per acre mentioned earlier. The cruel fact was that most of these displaced persons were not alive when the CM made this statement some times in 1988. In the context, Sri Sraddhakar Supakar once clarified the eighteen rupees and twelve annas per acre of land was the market value of the land in the year 1982 and on that basis the displaced persons were paid compensation in 1949 and in subsequent years.

The principle on the basis of which compensation was awarded to the oustees for their houses was more deceptive, illusory and arbitrary than the compensation awarded for their land. There was no proper market value of houses in the rural and tribal areas. Also, the houses were not treated as commercial commodities. In his report dated February 10, 1947, Mr. R.S. Sworn, the then Deputy Commissioner, Sambalpur had written about the amount of compensation to be paid for houses. Under the rules, compensation for houses and buildings was to be calculated on the cost of construction minus depreciation. Moreover, masonry buildings in rural areas had generally been constructed by the villagers for their residence and as such there was no market values for such buildings. Again houses in village bustees were seldom let out. No data regarding their real value was actually available. Huts were generally valued on plinth area at suitable rates to cover cost of construction, deduction being made for depreciation. The Hirakud project envisaged the acquisition of 163 villages with numerous hamlets. Notably, this note was prepared before arrival of a final decision to acquire a wider area covering about two hundred villages. If the land acquisition rules were strictly followed then compensation payable would not enable any house-owner to construct even one-fourth of his old plinth area under roofing. The cost of building materials had gone up by about three to four times and the rate of wages for unskilled and skilled labourers had shown similar increase. If the cost of buildings and hurts were evaluated at the prices of materials of the probable year of construction munus the cost of depreciation then the villagers well be hard hit.[17] In view of this Mr. Sworn divided the rural houses in to seven classes and suggested to fix the compensation amount at Rs. 250 only per pucca house with bricks or stone and line and masonry terraced roof. According to his report, the total estimated cost of about 17,690 houses came to nearly one crore thirty-five lakh forty thousand rupees.

Since February, 1949 the Government started works or rehabilitating the persons whose lands were acquired for the project. 600 acres of cultivable put unreclaimed land were reclaimed for the purpose of resettlement of displaced persons. Out of these, 200 acres were made ready for the purpose of cultivation by 1949. In reality, the villagers were not displaced by then and none of them came forward to take up cultivation in the reclaimed area. On experimental basis only six acres were taken up departmentally for the purpose of cultivation. But, there was not harvesting that year.[18] in response to a question putforth on March 13, 1950, the CM answered that the government had taken possession of Ac. 6567.18 decimals of land out of Ac. 31,501.76 decimals in the Hirakud area by the end of August, 1949. After six months, on September 13,1950, the CM informed to the house that State Government had taken possession of 10,553 acres of land and 572 acres were reclaimed by that time (See page 352 of the proceedings). In other words, the state government had made ready 572 acres when 10,553 acres were taken from the Hirakud oustees. Also these 572 acres were not distributed to the displaced persons who were deprived of their lands. Interestingly, the Government spent a sum of Rs. 17,960 toward cultivation of Ac. 126.50 decimals of reclaimed land. Black gram was sown and thirteen maunds was the total yield.[19] The price of this yield might be around three thousand rupees. What we went to emphasise here is that if a small or marginal farmer has to spend that much amount to get the above yield then he would be totally ruined in a single year.

It is learnt from the starred question no. 827, dated December 12, 1950 that 1490 acres were reclaimed with machines and 2467.76 acres were reclaimed by manual labour out of which only 324 acres were ready for cultivation. This might be an impressive figure from statistical point of view. But, in reality land in the jungle and wasteland which were to be allotted to the displaced persons for rehabilitation purpose were not completely prepared for cultivation. Just by cutting the standing trees from the land practically did not serve the purpose of cultivation. The poor quality of land preparation for rehabilitation purpose is attested by the following facts. In Sangramal Rehabilitation camp, 200 acres were prepared for paddy cultivation and 389 acres were prepared for cultivation of other crops. In 1951, experimental paddy cultivation in only three acres and seventy-five decimals of land yielded a meagre fifteen maunds and twenty-five seers. Answer to starred Question no. 485, dt. October 3, 1951 reveals that 9978.59 acres were reclaimed by the end of August, 1951 at a cost of Rs. 18,961,521, which was one hundred nine rupees per acre. In this context, one can realise the plight of a displaced person from Jamda village. One Bidyadhar Bhoi who received a sum of rupees twenty-one and four annas for a little more than one acre of land, came to the Sangramal camp and was allotted only twenty decimals of land which yielded only one maund of paddy per year. It would no be out of context to cite what the CM said earlier on March 13, 1950, "I repeat here what I said when I inaugurated the reclamation work in the village that if it so happens and I am sure it will not happen, if it so happens that land will not be reclaimed and people do not get enough time to build their houses elsewhere, no body will be turned out of their houses and their cultivation. No body will be made destitute. There is no single destitute today. No step will be taken which will make a single individual a destitute there."

In 1955 summer, people from more than fifty villages were driven out of their hearths and homes with the help of police power. The total submerged area was 59,215 acres of land out of which already cultivated areas was 39,595 acres and the remaining were cultivable land.[20] But, enough lands were not prepared even by that time for allotment to the displaced persons. Most of the displaced persons had earlier applied for land in the Rehabilitation centres and also deposited money for the purpose. They were asked to wait for land. But for how long?[21] Ultimately, money was refunded to the depositors because reclaimed lands were not readily available. It may be mentioned here that 1,47,363 acres of lands including valuable cultivable lands were submerged by July 1956, but by that time only 3790.20 acres were allotted to the Hirakud Oustees. Some 15000 families became homeless and landless, but only 1410 families were able to manage with this 3790.20 acres.[22] "When the then PM Sri Jawahar Nehru came to Preside over the opening ceremony of the Hirakud dam in January 1957, by that time the entire dam area was dazzling with electric light. But there was virtually no light to pave the way for these remaining thirteen thousand and five hundred displaced families. Had they not been fed with false promises, they could have made alternative arrangements earlier" was the common opinion of the Hirakud Oustees.

It would be unwise to say that government did not express its genuine concern over the welfare of displaced persons. Dr. Khosla proposed to construct model villages or colonies for the purpose of rehabilitation of the displaced people. As per the Hirakud Project Report, any expenditure on improvement of drinking water, electricity etc. which is in excess of the compensation allowance in the project should be met from the general revenue, as a contribution towards raising the standard of living of the displaced persons. The Central Water Irrigation and Navigation Commission (CWINC) prepared a plan of a model village/colony consisting of sixty houses at Larpank, situated nearly five Kms. away from Hirakud and seven Kms. away from Sambalpur. Total estimation to build that colony was Rs. 81,000. Significantly, the contractor who was awarded with this work was not paid the full amount because of the poor execution works. The then Governor of Orissa, Mr. Asaf Ali also inspected this colony or first model village for the Hirakud oustees and expressed his great displeasure. It was a matter of discussion even on the floor of Assembly. Reportedly, the villagers of Jamda were asked to go to the model village at Larpank. After verification, these landless, poor people expressed their desires that these houses should be provided to them free of cost.[23] Perhaps for this reason, they were not given house for house.

The above development may be analysed from the point of view of those twenty-four displaced families of Jamda village who combinedly received a merge amount of Rs. 513 only for about 28 acres of land. If the houses were meant for these displaced persons and for their rehabilitation, then the government should have realised that a landless person, because he was landless, would get nothing for land. At best, he could manage to get some two hundred and fifty rupees only for his house which was payable to the poorest type of house. As a matter of fact, these twenty-four families of Jamda village did lose 28 acres of land (by misfortune or carelessness of the state government?) but did not receive a single anna by the time the model village was completed. The government could not pay more than Rs. 250 for a single house acquired. More than five such houses were equivalent to a single house in the model village or colony at Larpank. Undoubtedly, a hefty amount of Rs. 81,000 was spent for the construction of sixty houses and each house was expected to cosat Rs. 1350 only. Notably, these 24 families (consisting of about 120 persons) who received Rs. 513 for 28 acres of land were not paid even half the price of a single house in the colony. To a man who had spent his life in a house in the submerged area, which the government had valued at Rs. 250, a house valued at Rs. 1350 in a colony could only be a white elephant. Moreover, there was no means of livelihood near the colony for these landless persons, who were once dependent on agriculture.

Depriving the people of their legitimate dues in respect of their houses was much easier than in case of their land. Land was a matter of record. Even after the lands were submerged, the land record of and oustee was a substantial evidence of the fact that he had a right to claim compensation for land. Allegedly, the Land Acquisition Office staff had to postpone the calculation and payment in respect of the house of an oustee till July, 1956 when the area was completely submerged. This was exactly what the government Officials wanted to happen.

Because, after the submergence it was difficult on the part of an oustee to establish that he had built a pucca house recently in the submerged area. In case of 163 villages, the Deputy Commissioner Mr. Swann had roughly calculated compensation for around 17,000 houses.

Reportedly, Dr. Khosla told the then CM[24] that he could complete the project in one year which was really a very short span of time. Unfortunately, it look almost ten years to complete the project. The Land Acquisition Establishment, the Reclamation and Rehabilitation organisations were in no hurry to complete the duties and responsibilities assigned to them. There was no time limit for this. Long after the submergence in 1956, the Officers continued to remain busy in calculating the compensation payable to the Hirakud oustees. Delay in calculation and payment of compensation did nothing but aggravated the woe of Hirakud oustees. In most cases, they had to compromise with the officials and accepted the lower amount of compensation. Whenever a to, Politician or bureaucrat visited Sambalpur he only praised for the patience of the Hirakud Land Organisation for its non-stop efforts of calculation of compensation. Even after thirty-two years in 1988, the CM[25] answered to a question that a sum of about fifteen lakhs rupees remained unpaid till then. And to-day after fifty years the CM[26] has again expressed concern over the fact that problems of the Hirakud Oustees are yet to be settled.

(The author is indebted to all of them who have been relentlessly fighting for the cause of the Hirakud Oustees. This paper is a tribute to memory of those fighters who have lost their lives unheard during the journey and process of their struggle for existence.)

REFERENCES

1. *The New Indian Express* (English Daily) Bhubaneswar , dt. 18.08.2001
2. *The Hirakud Dam Project Report* by Rai Bahadur A.N. Khosla, 1947, P. 113. The Hirakud Dam Project was conceived and prepared by Mr. Khosla in 1945 and the final report was published in June, 1947.

3. *The Hirakud Dam Project Report*, P. X
4. *Orissa Legislative Assembly Proceedings*, dt. 15.09.1946, P. 157.
5. *Orissa Legislative Assembly Proceedings*, dt. September 5, 1946.
6. At that time Sri Chintamani Mishra was the Director of Public Relations Department, Government of Orissa and Sri Balabhadra Panda was the D P R O, Sambalpur.
7. *Orissa Legislative Assembly Proceedings*, October 1950, P. 109.
8. Informations of Orissa Legislative Assembly Proceedings held sometimes in January, 1950 was supplied by Sri Sraddhakar Supakar (Ex-MLA) ;
9. Starred question no. 10, dt. 11.10. 1949.
10. The Editor of *The Prajatantra* (Oriya daily) was Sri H.K. Mahatab.
11. A.I.R. 1955 Orissa, 97 : The State of Orissa Vs. Bharat Chandra Nayak.
12. Starred question no. 2165, dt. 21.08.1955.
13. Starred question no. 132, dt. 8.12.1955.
14. Starred question dt. 21.11.1955 and dt. 13.12.1955.
15. Starred question no. 1782, dt. 25.09.1956.
16. Starred question no. 1912, dt. 29.05.1956.
17. *The Hirakud Dam Project Report*. 1947 Appendix XIII, P.318.
18. Starred question no.690, dt. 16.12.1949.
19. Starred question no. 2061, dt. 8.12.1950.
20. Starred question no. 2435, dt. 01.09.1955.
21. Starred question no. 2434, dt. 01.09.1955.
22. Starred question no. 1755, dt. 15.09.1956.
23. Starred question no. 26, dt. 04.03.1949.
24. At that time, the Chief Minister of Orissa was Dr. H.K. Mahatab.
25. At that time, the Chief Minister of Orissa was Sri Janaki Ballabh Pattnaik.
26. The Chief Minister of Orissa Sri Naveen Pattnaik.

10

The Political Economy of Development and Displacement

Dr. Deepak K. Mishra *

Alongwith the rate of economic growth, the distributive implications of growth has always remained at the centre of debates over development strategies. The exclusion of a large section of population from the process of economic development is no longer regarded as an exclusively distributive concern, its impact on overall growth prospects have also been realized. One of the important forms of exclusion and marginalization that arise out of large-scale development projects is the involuntary displacement of populations. Such displacements are 'frequent enough, big enough, complex and consequential enough to merit the full mobilization of conceptual, analytical and operational tools available to address it' (Carnea, 1996).

The present paper, apart from summarizing the findings of earlier studies on the nature, causes and implications of population displacement, attempts to develop a critique of the dominant paradigm within which the development-displacement interlinkages are generally analyzed. It has been argued that a historically informed understanding of the macro-processes of capital accumulation, environmental degradation and dispossession provides better insights into displacement and its manifold consequences. Displacement

* *Sr. Lecturer, Department of Economics, Arunachal University, Rono Hills, Itanagar-791 112 (A.P.).*

should be viewed not just as an abrupt event but as a process in this alternative framework.

Development, Displacement and Impoverishment: The Linkages

The rich and diverse discourse on displacement and rehabilitation, notwithstanding the differences in emphasis, has questioned the mainstream notions of industrialization-led development and has also attempted to articulate the rights of the displaced persons as citizens and human beings. Here our focus is on the most widely used framework for analyzing displacement and rehabilitation in the large and growing literature that can be called as 'displacement studies'.

Displacement is generally viewed as an undesirable but inevitable outcome of the development projects initiated by the state. Often, displacement is defined as the process of expropriation of land and other assets in order to allow a *project* to proceed for the *overall social good* (Sinha, 1996, emphasis added). Conceptually, a distinction is made between involuntary and voluntary migration of populations. It is argued that voluntary mobility, including rural-urban migration results from both push and pull factors. Essentially, such mobility reflects people's willingness and ability to shift to new and better opportunities and is considered natural and desirable in the course of economic transformation and growth. On the other hand, involuntary mobility or displacement is a result of push factors alone. The age composition of the migrant population is also different in the two cases. While, the people who migrate voluntarily are generally young families in the early stages of their household life cycle, entire populations are forced to move in the case of involuntary displacement. Again, in the case of voluntary mobility migration is usually a gradual process in the sense that social and economic ties with the village is maintained and it serves as a safety net in the face of adverse circumstances in a new and alien environment. Forced migration is marked by a disruption of diverse risk-sharing and social insurance mechanisms (Guggenheim and Carnea, 1995). Often a distinction between disaster-induced displacement and development-induced displacement is also emphasized. In case of displacements caused by calamities like flood, cyclone, famine and war, it is generally possible for people to return to their original places of residence after a short period and hence short-term relief measures assumes importance in the rehabilitation package. Development-induced displacement is permanent and hence it necessitates a different and long-term rehabilitation assistance (Thukral, 1992; Asthana, 1996).

While the causes of displacement, in the sense defined above, is regarded as diverse and complex, the types of projects and interventions that are cited as the major causes of large-scale dislocation of populations are: hydro-power and multipurpose dam projects (particularly large dams), mines (particularly open cast mines), super thermal and nuclear power plants, industries, military installations, weapon-testing grounds, ports, railways and highways, the notification and expansion of reserved forest areas, sanctuaries and parks (Carnea, 1996; Thukral, 1992; Pandey, 1998; Fernandes and Thukral, 1989). The large and growing literature on the effects of displacement caused by various developments initiatives in Post-Independence India has conclusively demonstrated the irreversible, catastrophic and disruptive implications of such large-scale displacement (Kothari, 1996; Thukral, 1992; Mathur & Marsden, 1998; D' Souza et al., 1998; Patnaik, 2000; Chaudhary, 2000; Mohapatra, 1998, 2000). Some of the major conclusions of these studies are:

(i) The government simply does not have complete information on the number of persons displaced by various projects. The estimates for the period 1991 to 1996 range from a conservative 110 lakhs to an overall figure of 185 lakhs. If project affected persons and victims of secondary displacements are added, the figure becomes as high as four crores (Kothari, 1996);

(ii) Among all the development projects large dams are the single largest cause of displacement;

(iii) Tribals are disproportionately affected by developmental displacement. The 29th Report of the Commissioner of Scheduled Castes and Tribes notes that even though tribals are roughly 7.5 per cent of the population, over 40 per cent of those displaced till 1990 came from these communities. The proportion of tribals among those displaced is not only high but it has been increasing as well;

(iv) Among the displaced people women, children and the aged were more adversely affected. Landless labourers, small and marginal farmers and artisans were worse affected in many cases;

(v) Most of these development projects were not planned on the basis of a comprehensive cost-benefits analysis. Even in the cases where such exercises were undertaken the social and environmental costs were not properly calculated (Morse and Berger, 1992).

These studies have identified a number of harmful effects of displacement, which include: dismantling of productive systems, disruption of local labour markets, disruption of trade and market links, deskilling of the labour force, disempowerement, scattering of kinship groups and family systems, weakening of self-management and social control, disorganization of informal social networks that provide mutual support, loss of complex social relationships which provide avenues for representation, mediation and conflict-resolution, loss of ancestral sacred-zones, graves and places of worships, psychological stress and mental health problems (Carnea, 1996, 2000; Kothari, 1996; Good, 1996; Patnaik, 2000; Chaudhuri, 1998). Such displacement starts processes that generate spirals of impoverishment.

The Impoverishment, Risk and Reconstruction (IRR) Framework: A Critique

One of the most well known conceptual frameworks to study displacement and rehabilitation is the model developed by a leading World Bank consultant and policy analyst Michael Carnea (Carnea, 1996, 1998, 2000). His model has been used and operationalized by many scholars while studying displacement and rehabilitations in different contexts. (Pandey, 1998; Mahapatra, 1998). The model, called the Impoverishment, Risk and Rehabilitation Model, is basically an analytical framework drawing upon a number of earlier studies. It identifies a set of key variables that create or accentuate impoverishment risks and analyses their inter-connections during involuntary displacement. This understanding is extended to develop a framework for reconstruction of livelihood of re-settlers. Despite the enormous diversity of project-specific situations, the various kinds of risks that threaten the survival of the displaced persons are landlessness, joblessness, homelessness, marginalization, food insecurity, increased morbidity and mortality, loss of common property resources and services and social disarticulation. These impoverishment risks, emphasizes Carnea, 'must be seen in their interconnectedness, as a pattern of variables' (Carnea, 2000). These risks are not distributed evenly. Gender-sensitive analysis reveals that women suffer more than men do. Children and elderly people share a disproportionately higher burden of these risks. He also recognizes the risk to the host population-risks like increasing pressure in land and other resources, employment loss, price rise, environmental degradation and cultural clashes, because of re-settlement efforts. On the basis of identified basic risks and their inter-connectedness, Carnea suggests a framework for reconstruction, in his framework are land-based re-settlement, reemployment, gains in living standards through improved housing conditions, and also an imaginative programme of community reconstruction, social inclusion and restoration of CPRs.

The numerous micro studies on displacement experiences in various parts of the country have definitely broadened our understanding of the process of deprivation and marginalization created by large-scale human dislocation. Their cumulative impact has been to bring out the fallacies of the main steam models of economic growth into closer scrutiny. Nevertheless, inspite of recognizing the similarities in the impact of various development projects, the IRR framework, for example, accepts such projects as inevitable and then considers its implications. The various rounds of displacements are generally conceptualized as repetitive but distinct events.

Even when it is recognized that displacement is a process, its starting point is made out to be the day the official process for land acquisition starts. This restricted view not only leaves many other forms of displacement outside the scope of analysis (some of which will be discuss latter on) but also limits the analytical framework to the effect that many crucial casual mechanisms are excluded from the discussion.

Firstly, to define displacement as physical dislocation caused by development projects in general and mega projects in particular is to de-emphasize the structural and historical character of the development process. There are many cases where people are displaced not because of an abrupt mega event like construction of a dam or a power plant but through a slow and painful process of deliberate undermining of the natural, economic and institutional basis of their survival. These processes like changes in land and water management systems, ecological degradation, pollution of water bodies, the establishment of mono cultures in land, in water and in forest are also the result of the so-called development process and their impacts on people, if judged in proper perspective, are no less catastrophic. A few studies have also shown that commercialization as a process also uproots people from their sources of livelihood. The project-induced-displacement framework fails to recognize these diverse patterns of displacement. Some of these can not be attributed specific projects but are result of a specific pattern of development. Sometimes scholars have attempted to include some of these displacements, through categories like *'secondary displacement'*, *'project affected persons'*, and *'ecological refugees'*. But the problem can not be solved by creating new and additional categories of displaced people rather the real challenge is to create a framework of analysis that can adequately explain the processes through which such diverse forms of displacements take place.

Secondly, the displacement-rehabilitation studies are generally conceptualized in a state versus – people framework. To be sure, some of these studies are based on sophisticated and nuanced understanding of the political economy of development and state intervention in an underdeveloped economy, but a majority to them treat displacement as an outcome of state interventions alone. This may be because of the fact that land for both public and private projects are acquired by state departments and in either case it is the state which is expected to pay the compensation. However, displacement is the ultimate outcome of a process of economic transformation, natural resources extraction and profit generation. By questioning the role of state in the process, these studies have definitely undermined the idea of a neutral, benevolent or pro-poor state, but at the class character of the development initiatives. Apart from that, this framework of analyzing displacement will face serious problems in the emerging scenario under globalization and liberalization. The Draft National Policy of Rehabilitation, prepared in 1996 by the Ministry of Rural Development in its opening paragraph admits that with the advent of New Economic Policy, it is expected that 'there will be large-scale investments both on account of internal generation of capital and increased inflow of foreign investments, their by creating an enhanced demand for land *to be provided within a short time span* in an increasingly competitive market-led economic structure'. That the causes and dimensions of future and ongoing displacements can not be properly analyzed without incorporating the changing dynamics of global capital accumulation can hardly be over emphasized.

Most of the policy oriented studies, like the IRR framework itself, generally accept displacement as given and then work towards a better rehabilitation package, so as to minimise resistance to the project. Carnea's IRR model in fact does not allow to raise the fundamental questions about the desirability of the projects.

Displacement as a Process: Towards an Alternative Formulation

What follows is basically a preliminary attempt to suggest an alternative framework for analyzing phenomena like displacement. The starting point is the explicit recognition of the fact that the debate on displacement, project induced or otherwise, is not just about a comparison between aggregate costs and benefits but also about the distribution of such costs and benefits among individuals, classes and communities. When the desirability or otherwise of investment decisions or changes in resource-use patterns are decided in a structured, hierarchical and class-divided society, political economy is probably the proper analytical framework to begin with.

Old fashioned as it may sound, some fundamental confusions can be avoided if we start from the classical writing on dispossession. In his discussion on primitive accumulation, Marx has categorically stated that *'capitalism presupposes the complete separation of labourers from all property by which they can realize their labour'*. The history of this expropriation, through which peasant-producers and others become free-labourers in the double sense of the term, notes Marx, is written in the annals of mankind in the letters of blood and fire. He was aware that the history of this expropriation in different countries, assumes different aspects, and runs through its various phases in different orders of succession, and at different periods. But his basic point was that dispossession of independent producers from their means of production is a fundamental precondition for the commodification of labour-power, which in turn is essential for capitalism in its classic form to develop. His chapter on *'The Modern Theory of Colonization'*, bring out the argument more forcefully. Refuting the bourgeois thesis that capital (a thing) originated in the fruitful exercise of the producer's own capacity of labour, while labour-power as a commodity arose through a voluntary social contract, Marx cites the role of legislation and force to prevent migrant workers in the colonies to be owners of the means of production. Because, as long as *'labour can accumulate for himself and this he can do as long as the remain possessor of his means of production-capitalist accumulation and capitalist mode of production are impossible'*. To cite these arguments is not to emphasize that dispossession and what is often called displacement has its historical roots. Notwithstanding the unevenness in the spatial dynamics of capital accumulation large scale displacements are not simply the undesirable, unintended and unfortunate consequences of otherwise beneficial projects, they are the essential and defining features of capitalist expansion in an underdeveloped economy. Displacement or dispossession as a process does not start with establishment of specific projects, in fact what is conventionally called displacement is only the more brutal, abrupt and large-scale manifestations of an ongoing process of pauperization and creation of proletarians during capitalist reconstruction.

Capital enters into underdeveloped regions for broadly three different interests: (i) raw materials (ii) market and (iii) strengthening state power. In this process the pre-capitalist social formation are differentiated, but the degree and character of differentiation may not follow an uniform pattern (Rao, 1995). If we look at the different projects or 'sources' of displacement, even in the conventional framework, most of them are necessary primarily to serve the interests of capital in all the three dimensions, which are not necessarily mutually exclusive. But apart from such extractive activities, infrastructural projects and establishment of military-industrial complexes, we can also analyze a number of other processes, which are ultimately results of capitalist expansion in to tribal areas. Not all of them are direct, visible and immediate in terms of their effects but the brutal similarities in their impacts are the dispossession and dislocation of the population.

The other crucial dimension of this alternative framework being suggested is the necessity to bring in the historical dimension of the problem. One of the crucial features of many displacement studies is their blatant negligence of this dimension. The dynamics of capitalist expansion can be fruitfully analyzed only on the basis of the historical evolution of the social formations with all their specificities and peculiarities. A historical understanding of the changes in the modes and relation of production, the property-rights regimes, the modes of resource-use and extraction are essential to analyze the dynamics of dispossession, marginalization and dislocation.

The other conceptual building block in this framework is the *ecological* dimensions of capitalist expansion. The starting point is to recognize that the crisis of environment is not a crisis of nature but a crisis of society. John Bellamy Foster, has argued that 'the causes of environmental destruction that faces us today are not biological or the products of individual human-choice. They are social and historical, rooted in the productive relations, technological imperatives, and historically conditioned demographic trends that characterize the dominant social system' (Foster, 1994). To emphasize the link between environmental degradation and capitalism is not to assume that all non-capitalist social formations were free from the problem, but to remind ourselves that with the onslaught of capitalism 'some sort of hegemonic economic-engineering discourse has come to dominate the discussion of environmental questions, commodifying everything and subjecting all transactions, to the singular logic of commercial profitability and cost benefit calculus' (Harvey, 1998: 23). The expansionary drive of capitalism has transformed the modes of resources use over the entire world and some of its harmful effects are global, but it is also important to note that environmental impacts frequently have a *social bias.* And because of this underdeveloped countries and regions, weaker sections and marginalized groups are frequently made victims of this ecocide. The processes of dispossession, extinction and environmental destruction are being *exported* to the third world under the name of *globalization.* The links between slow or abrupt dislocation of population in underdeveloped countries and regions of the world needs to be understood in the context of this aggressive expansionary drive of global capitalism in the post-cold-war period.

Concluding Remarks

The central argument of the paper may be summarized as follows: the conceptualization of displacement as an unintended and unavoidable outcome of an otherwise beneficial process of economic development is fundamentally flawed. Displacement has to be seen in the large dynamics of capital accumulation and consequent dispossession. The problem of involuntary displacement is intrinsically related to the nature of capitalist development and hence instead of analyzing it as repetitive but district events, it is better to conceptualize displacement as a process. The abrupt, large-scale involuntary population displacements are only the more violent forms of this process. Alongwith them the slow but equallv catastrophic processes of dispossession need to be analyzed to understand displacement as a process. Recent shift towards a market-led development strategy, to the extent that it signifies increasing corporate control over resources and economic opportunities, has crucial implication for the survival and livelihood of a large section of people living in the developing world. Its magnitude and implications can be properly judged only when the linkages between macro-economic restructuring and dispossession of subsistence producers are explicitly recognized. Needless to say, the impact of globalization and neo-liberal policies on poverty, inequality and environment will have a crucial bearing on the process of displacement in coming decades.

Acknowledgement

[An earlier version of the paper was presented in a Seminar on 'Internal Displacement in the Arunachal Pradesh', organized by the Department of History, Arunachal University on November 21-22, 2000. The author is grateful to participants. The usual disclaimers apply.]

REFERENCES

1. Carnea, Michael M. (1996) 'Public Policy Response to Population Displacements' *Economic and Political Weekly*, Vol. 31, No. 24
2. Carnea, Michael M. (1998) 'Impoverishment or Social Justice? A Model for Planning Resettlement' in Mathur and Marsden (1998).
3. Carnea, Michael M. (2000) 'Risks, Safeguards and Reconstruction: A Model for Population Displacement', *Economic and Political Weekly*, Vol. 35, No. 41.
4. Sinha, B.K. (1996) 'National Policy for Rehabilitation: Objectives and Principles', *Economic and Political Weekly*, Vol. 31, No. 24.
5. Ganguly-Thukral, E. (1996) 'Development, Displacement and Rehabilitation: Locating Gender', *Economic and Political Weekly*, Vol. 31, No. 24.
6. ---------- (ed) (1992) '*Big Dams, Displaced People: Rivers of Sorrow, Rivers of Change*, Sage, New Delhi.
7. Good Byron. J. (1996) Mental Health Consequences of Displacement and Resettlement, *Economic and Political Weekly*, Vol.31, No. 24.
8. Pandey, B. (1998) *Displaced Development: Impact of Open Cast Mining on Women*, Friedrich Ebert Stiftung, New Delhi.
9. Fernades, Walter and Enakshi Ganguly Thukral (1989) *Development, Displacement and Rehabilitation*, Indian Social Institute, New Delhi.
10. Asthana, R. (1996) 'Involuntary Resettlement: International Experience', *Economic and Political Weekly*, Vol. 31, No. 24.
11. Harvey, David (1998) 'The Geography of the Manifesto' in Panitach, Leo and Colin Leys (ed) *Socialist Registrar* 1998, Merlin.
12. Foster, John Bellamy (1994) '*The Vulnerable Planet: A Short Economic History of the Environment*, Monthly Review Press, New York (Indian Reprint: 1999).
13. Morse, Bradford and Berger Thomas (1992) '*Sardar Sarovar: The Report of the Independent Review*, Indian Reprint.
14. Mathur, Harimohan and David Marsden (Eds.) (1998) *Development Projects and Impoverishment Risks: Resettling Project Affected People in India*, Oxford University Press, Delhi.
15. Ramaiah, Savitri (1998) *Impact of Involuntary Resettlement on Levels of living in*: Mathur and Marsden (1998).
16. Chaudhuri, S.K. (1998) 'Development and Displacement: Anthropological Perspective' In : Srivastava, S.P. (ed) *The Development Debate: Critical Perspectives*, Rawat Publications, Jaipur.
17. D'Souza Rohan, P. Mukhopadhyay and Ashish Kothari (1998) 'Re-Evaluating Multi-Purpose River Valley Projects: A case-study of Hirakud, Ukai and IGNP', *Economic and Political Weekly*, Vol. 33, No. 6.
18. Mohapatra, L.K. (2000) 'Resettlement with Participation, The Indian Experience', *The Eastern Anthropologist*, Vol. 53, Nos. 1-2.

19. Kothari, S. (1996) 'Whose National? Displaced as Victims of Displacement', *Economic and Political Weekly*, Vol. 31, No. 24.
20. Rao, R. S. (1995) *Towards Understanding Semi-Feudal Semi-Colonial Society*, Perspective, Hyderabad.
21. Mahapatra, L. K. (1998) 'Good Intentions or Policies are not Enough Reducing Impoverishment Risks for the Tribal Oustee', In: Mathur and Marsden (1998).
22. Patnaik, S.M. (2000) 'Understanding Involuntary Resettlement: An Anthropological perspective', *The Eastern Anthropologist*, Vol. 53, Nos. 1-2

11

Displacement and Development: A Cost Benefit Analysis

— *Dr. Surendra Nath Behera* * *& Smt. Ranjita Kumari Mohanty* **

Infrastructure development through major industrial power generation, irrigation and water management projects has become an integral part of sustained and self generating process of economic development. Strengthening of Social and Economic Overheads in the form of transport, communication, power etc. are considered imperative for augmenting agricultural and industrial productivity increasing employment potential and income generation. A large number of Irrigation-cum-power Projects have been undertaken in the post-independence period for agricultural and industrial development of the country. Basic heavy and strategic industries such as iron, steel, fertilizers and chemicals inhabitants. Large scale mining operation in the tribal areas have displaced the tribal inhabitants causing a negative spill over costs. Construction of railway lines, irrigation canals etc. have caused numerous burden of miseries to the inhabitants in terms loss of cultivable land and consequential agricultural productivity.

Social Cost of Displacement

Installation of different projects have caused diversity of negative externalities beyond the market transaction process.

---

* *Reader and Head, Department of Economics, D. D. Colleges, Keonjhar, Orrisa 758001.*

** *Lecturer in Economics, Govt. Women's College, Keonjhar, Orissa–758001.*

The Third Party effects `or' Negative neighborhood effects must be taken into account in evaluation of Public sector projects and application of efficiency criteria to public expenditure. The spill over costs or external costs on the society are direct and indirect, tangible and intangible and monetary and real to be assessed in a comprehensive manner in making feasibility studies . Though people have been displaced systematically because of development projects, there is loss of concern and seriousness in computing the number of `Oustees' not to speak of the Project-affected Persons. The Development-induced displacement Process have been directly hit by the projects in terms of problems faced in rehabilitation and resettlement.

Multi-purpose Projects

The Multipurpose projects aim at improvement of irrigation facility, generation of hydroelectricity for domestic, agricultural and industrial purposes. Projects set up in tribal areas have the severity of displacement effect on the tribals. When the Upper Kolab Multi-purpose Project in Koratput District of Orissa was commissioned it was recognised an area of 29,788.60 acres of submergence, displacing 3067 families out of which 1443 were Scheduled Tribes, 458 Schedules Castes and 1166 belonging to other categories. Families were displaced from 51 villages and two hamlets. The National Commission on Scheduled Castes and Scheduled Tribes listed displacement of 3106 families from 44 villages of which 1532 were Scheduled Tribes. Similarly the World Bank Staff Appraisal Report in 1983 stated that about 20,000 people residing in 105 hamlets in Koraput and Kalahandi districts were displaced of which most of them were tribals. Irrigation Projects have inevitably caused acquisition of land for the purpose and loss of agricultural productivity.

Mines

In the mines area, there is a greater tribal concentration. It is observed that people taking the lease of iron ore, manganese, chromite etc. have to clear the forest area before starting the digging or drilling operations. The displacement effect and social. Costs of the Mines are measured in terms of ecological imbalance, environmental degradation, heavy toll on the wild life and health hazards to the workers and inhabitants of the neighborhood area. Though the legal provisions exist for creation of forest area by plantation equivalent to the forest area cleared for mining operations, those are not strictly adhered to. Further the tribal people depending on the minor forest products called as Non-Timber Forest Produce (NTFP) lose their sources of livelihood through collection of different produces such as firewood, fodder, timber and other NTFPs such as tamarind, Sal leaves, Kendu leaves, honey, oil seeds, forest fruits and nuts, Jhuna, Khajuri pata, herbal medicine etc. Since there is a greater dependence on forests in collecting NTFPs for domestic consumptions and sale in the market. Mining operations as well as mineral-based industries using inputs from the mines have to pay adequate compensation for the sufferers.

The tribal inhabitants still restore the traditional age-old occupations like `shifting cultivation' which provided them with a large variety of crops, cereals, pulses, oilseeds and vegetables. Projects undertaken in these areas have adversely affected their life support system. The Juanga, Mundas and Gonds depend upon forests and mountain ranges for their livelihood.

Dams and Minor Irrigation Projects

Construction of Dams and Minor Irrigation Projects (MIPs) have been felt imperative in the hilly and dry land areas. Conservation of water resources and using them for agricultural operations has been made in many areas. However, the displacement effect of these Projects are felt in coverage of cultivable land by water and consequent agriculture output and loss of habitation.

Industries

Infrastructure development in the form of provision of power, transport and railways have the displacement impact on villages habitations and cultivable land area. Dr. Walter Frenandes in 1992 report submitted to the ICSSR on Development–induced Displacement in the Tribal areas of Eastern India in his Conservating Estimate of persons displaced by various categories showed that number of persons displaced by industries is 13,00,000 of which only 3,25,000 constituting 25% were rehabilitated keeping a Backlog of rest 75%.

Social Benefits Areas

The social benefits of the Projects undertaken includes both real and pecuniary which may be both direct and indirect tangible and intangible intermediate and final and outside.

Real benefits are derived by the final consumers of the Public Project and reflect and addition to community welfare Pecuniary benefits are assessed in terms of changes in relative prices of factors and products and increased earning. Direct benefits and costs are those related to the main project objective while indirect benefits are in the nature of by products. Thus a river development programme may have flood control as the immediate objective but may also have important bearings on the supply of water, on irrigation or on soil erosion in adjacent areas.

While tangible benefits and costs are evaluated in terms of market prices, intangibles in the form of its effects on health and living standard of community welfare are assessed using 'Shadow Prices' or 'Accounting Prices'.

Simultaneously, while intermediate benefits help in the production of other goods, final benefits are provision of final goods to the consumers.

Benefits are also internal or inside and external or outside. Thus flood control measures taken in one area also prevent flood in the download areas. They are external or spill over from one jurisdiction to another.

The following is an illustration of Projects Benefits and Costs in evaluation of efficiency criteria of public expenditure to an Irrigation Project:

		Benefits	Costs
Real			
Direct	Tangible	Increased farm output	Cost of Pipes
	Intangible	Beautification of area	Loss of Widerness
Indirect	Tangible	Reduced soil erosion	Diversion of Water
	Intangible	Preservation of rural society	Destruction of Wild life
Pecuniary	Relative Improvement in position of farm equipment industry.		

The ratio of Net Present Value of the Projects (NPVP) on the benefit Cost-ratio provides a measure of economic feasibility of the project. In case of a single project, it is choosen it its B/C ratio is one or greater than one. In case of many competing projects ranking of projects are made in descending order on the basis of $\frac{B}{C}$ or $\frac{B - C}{C}$.

Internal rate of return is to be used taking into account the future uncertainties so that Present Value = Future value x discounting factors

discounted to present worth involving time factor for evaluation. Social marginal productivity of a project is evaluated by deducting social opportunity cost of displaced persons from the marginal product.

SMP = MP – Social opportunity cost.

Displacement and Compensation

The process of rehabilitation of the 'Oustees' starts by calculating the loss of assets and source of income lost do that compensation is to be paid as per the legal provisions. A landless labour or artisan without homestead or house in his name is not entitled to get any compensation under existing laws of rehabilitation. Occupants and cultivators without any legal document of possession individual ownership will not be entitled to nay compensation. Tribals adopting shifting cultivation and oustees staying for a long time were not classified as displaced persons for rehabilitation purposes and securing compensation. There is imperative need to pay compensation to both the dwellers in revenue villages with right to land and others lived for a longer period and governed by forest laws. Exploitation of resources of the forest which threatens the very survival of the forest dwellers and the denial of equivalent compensation is violation of the constitutional provisions of fundamental rights. Article 12.3 enjoins upon Government that 'persons thus removed shall be fully compensated for any resulting loss or injury'. The customary rights of the tribal people are on individual rights on planted or land occupied or collective rights on trees planted deserve compensation. Adequate and timely compensation is the first step in the process of rehabilitation and resettlement of the displaced population.

Rehabilitation & Resettlement of the Displaced Persons – The Policy Imperatives

The available rehabilitation policy provides guidelines of rehabilitation and compensation. Rehabilitation of the tribals must be given priority and should form an integral part of mining, irrigation, forest and wild life projects. At least one member from each displaced family must be given employment as a source of livelihood. Displaced people, particularly tribals showed be encouraged to set up ancillary units and must be provided entrepreneurial training.

The cost of rehabilitation must include training cost for absorbing displaced tribals. Support services around the main project need to be provided such as fishery, carpentry, dairy, poultry, and other vocational opportunities. While alloting land to the affected people smaller irrigation projects should be taken up for agricultural rehabilitation.

Forest dwellers and persons living on minor forest products, foodgatherers, shifting cultivators and tribals artisans should be rehabilitated near the forest to which they are psychologically and economically adapted.

Free houses or concessional loan for house construction should be provided along with community facilities like schools, roads, drinking water, primary health care in the pattern of Dandakaranya Development Authority evolved by the Ministry of Rehabilitation.

Adequacy of compensation should be provided on the basis of replacement value of the land to be acquired in the area of resettlement and not on the basis of area of displacement. Projects affected persons must be given adequate life-support system. For proper computation of the assets of the illiterate and ignorant tribals both Govt. and Non-Govt. organisations should be created among their mind. The area of resettlement must be choosed giving priority of choice of the displaced in the periphery.

Hence, there is an imperative need for a rational Rehabilitation Policy. Forced displacement should be avoided as far as possible. The planners and the administrators should not impose the unilateral process of development on the innocent and voiceless people. In a Welfare State adequate consideration must be given to 'Social Cost and Human Costs' in the development process. Any process of development should not lead to deprivation of the legitimate rights in establishing industrial projects. There is need for balanced reconciliation between displacement and resettlement. Maximisation of communal welfare with minimum hardship to the displaced should be the goals of development policy. In the name of high development ideals the life of the displaced should not be at stake. The thrust of the new development strategy is to maximise a definite social welfare function within the constraints of minimum unavoidable displacement cost. The projects are to implemented with the full involvement of the locals those will receive benefits within short time frame.

REFERENCES

1. G. Scott, *Development and Dynamics of Displacement*, Institute for Social and Economic Change, Bangalore 1990.
2. L.K. Mohapatra, *Tribal Development in India–Myth and Reality*, Vikas Publishing House, New Delhi, 1997.
3. W. Fernandes & E.G. Thukral (Eds.), *Development, Displacement and Rehabilitation*, Indian Social Institute, New Delhi.
4. A.K. Dasgupta & D.W. Pearce, *Cost Benefits Analysis, Theory and Practice*, 1978.
5. A.R. Prest & R. Turvey, *Cost Benefit Analysis—A Survey*, American Economic Association
6. Sudgen and Williams, *The Principles of Practical Cost Benefit Analysis* Oxford University Press, 1978.

12

Problems of Displacement and Development

*— Dr. S. N. Tripathy **

The important aims of river dam projects were controlling floods, generating electricity and providing facilities of irrigation. During last one hundred years, there were 4291 large river dam projects started. Because of these river dam projects about 11.5 crores of people have been displaced. According to Central Water Commission at an average 24,535 hectares of land have been submerged by water by 54 river dam projects. According to Indian Institute of Public Administration—which collected data on 213 river dam projects reveals that per each river dam project at an average 8,748 hectares of land have been displaced by these 213 river dam projects. The data collected from 34 river dam projects reveal the fact that out of displaced people 47% are tribals. The volume of displaced people by all type of developmental projects are much higher than river projects. According to the World Refugee Survey (2000) the magnitude of industrially displacement of people in India was 5,07,000, whereas the Indian Social Institute, New Delhi estimated total as 21.3 million, out of which displaced due to dams constitute 16.4 million, mines 2,55 million, Industrial development 1.25 million, Wild-life sanctuaries 7 million and National Park 0.6 million (Fernades, 1994).[1]

The number of population displaced by different developmental projects in India since the commencement of

---

* *Dr. Tripathy, Dept. of Economics, Aska Science College.*

five year plan till 1990 stood at around 1.85 crs. (Table 1).

Table 1
Displacement of Population by Development Projects (1981-90)

S. No.	Projects	Number of Projects	Year	Displaced Population
1.	Large Dams	2422	1990	1,40,000.00
2.	Mines	1210	1983	21,000.00
3.	Industries	—	1990	13,000.00
4.	Parks & Sanctuary	468	1990	6,000.00
5.	Others	—	—	5,000.00
	Total			1,85,000.00

Source: Development, Displacement and Rehabilitation in Tribal Areas of Orissa (1992), Indian Social Institute, New Delhi.

According to the World Commission on Dams (WCD) by India Country Study (ICS), during 1980 to 2000, the major river dams have submerged 91 lakh hectares of forests.

Table 2 demonstrates the displaced population as well as the tribal displaced population due to the river dam projects in India.

It is found that the displaced population was 15,000 during 1979 which increased to two lakh twenty thousand by 1995. About 90% of displaced people in various dam projects have not been provided justice. During last 50 years, in various dams about 6 crores of population have been displaced. Out of these 6 crores, 4 crores have virtually become beggars in the street. On the contrary, despite these dams, due to improper utilization of dam water only 10% of agricultural land of India could yield crops.

The Narmada Valley Project (NVP) is the largest multipurpose river project in India. The NVP aims to provide water to the drought prone districts of Sourastra, Kutch, North Gujarat and some parts of Rajasthan. At 1988 base index, the

NVP will cost the exchequer about Rs. 5000 crores and displace about over 1 million people. It will submerge over 37,000 hectares of land. It will cause a loss of standing forests over worth Rs. 30,000 crores. In this context it is mention-worthy that, "In a majority decision, with two judges including the Chief Justice of India in favour of the Narmada Project and one member of the Apex Court dissenting, the Supreme Court has ruled that construction work on the dam up to a height of 90 meters be taken up immediately."

Table 2

River Dam Projects and Displaced Population

Projects	State	Displaced Population	Displaced Tribal People
01	02	03	04
Curzen	Gujarat	11,600	100%
Sardar Sarovar	Gujarat	2,00,000	57.06%
Maheswar	Madhya Pradesh	20,000	60%
Dhabaghat	Madhya Pradesh	13,000	73.91%
Ichha	Bihar	30,800	80%
Chandil	Bihar	37,600	87%
Koelkar	Bihar	66,000	88%
Mohibajaj Sagar	Rajasthan	38,400	76.28%
Polbharam	Andhra Pradesh	1,50,000	52.90%
Mythan	Bihar	93,870	56.46%
Upper Indravati	Orissa	18,500	89.20%
Ichhampali	Himachal Pradesh	38,100	76.28%
Tultil	Andhra Pradesh	13,600	51.61%
Domanganga	Gujarat	8,700	48.70%
Bhakra	Himachal Pradesh	36,000	34.36%
Manas	Bihar	3,700	31.00%
Bhalkar	Gujarat	52,000	18.92%

Source: The Pragatibadi, The Oriya Daily, Dated 27.12.2000.

Significantly, the reason for clearance of the Project is based on the Court's satisfaction at the manner in which the relief and rehabilitation of these ousted by the dam are being undertaken. This is the one issue of which the Narmada Bachao Andolan (NBA) has created a country-wide movement, drawing attention of the misery and plight of those displaced so far and these likely to be ousted with the planned increase in the height of the structure (The Times of India, 14.11.2000).

The NBA needs to be congratulated for bringing to public attention an issue which has generally been neglected in the past while implementing many public or private sector projects. It has been manifested that some ousted families were constrained to move as many as six times. This is a cruel state of affair on the significance we attention we attach to the human dimension of a problem.

The most negative impact of Narmada Dam Project will be felt by Madhya Pradesh, which would have to rehabilitate the largest number of person likely to be displaced. The power generation from the Narmada Dam Project would hardly be significant with a capacity of 1,450 MW.

In this context, Pachauri (2000)[2] has aptly remarked, "If indeed the only means of getting water in areas of Gujarat and Rajasthan that are chronically water scarce is through this Project, then what weightage due are attach to this benefits vis-a-vis the acute misery of being ousted in Madhya Pradesh? There is clearly a case of uneven costs and benefits to which there are no simple answers, and hence the sharply divergent position on the subject between Gujarat and Madhya Pradesh."

Development Induced Displacement in Orissa

According to official estimates the total number of families displaced due to river dam projects and other development projects in Orissa between 1950-1993 was 81,176 of which 80 per cent families have been displaced due to irrigation projects only (Pandey, 2000)[3]. During the said period mining activities have displaced 3,145 thousands, industries, 10,704, thermal power 2,426 and dams 64,903. In a official estimate only Hirakud dam has displaced around 40 thousand people, but other study demonstrate the number of displaced persons over 180 thousand. The picture relating to displaced families due to various development project in Orissa can be found from the Table 3.

Table 3

S. No.	Name of the Project	Displaced Families	ST/SC Families
1.	Balimela Multi-purpose dam project on Sileru river at Chitrakonda.	2000	
2.	Salandi Irrigation Project	589	552 tribals families.
3.	Rengali Multi-purpose river valley project on the Brahmani river in Angul District.	10,897	1,710 SC families 1172 ST families.
4.	Upper Kolab Multi-purpose dam project on the river Kolab in Koraput District.	3,179	442 SC families 1421 ST families.
5.	Upper Indravati Multi-purpose project.	5,301	2223 families Triblas 796 families SC.
6.	Rourkela Steel Plant.	4,251	—
7.	Talcher Coal belt region in Angul District.	23 villages affected by underground mines due to open cast mining project 38 villages.	—
8.	IB valley area in Jharsuguda District.	17 villages affected and 130 families displaced due to five open cast mining.	—

Source: Pandey, Balaji (1998), Depriving the underprevileged by Development, Bhubaneshwar.

Problem involved in Compensation Payment

Displacement because of long-term projects, like construction of a reservoir, power plant, industry and mining may take over an area displacing the inhabitants. This involuntary displacement or development induced displacement with a view to achieve accelerated economic development through various investment projects necessitates vast amount of land. This land acquisition for public interest and national building are made through the payment of compensation to the owner of land or housing property etc.

Prof. G.C. Kar (1999)[4] remarks, "When ownership rights become the only point in determining compensation then three disadvantageous situations may arise:

(i) What about those who do not own land individually? In many tribal communities land is held by the community families are given the right to cultivate. The arrangement is oral–between the tribal Chief and the family and, no record is maintained.

(ii) What about those do not own land either individually or as a community but depend on land for a living? The landless agricultural laborers belong to this category.

(iii) What about those who are no land owners and yet cultivate land? Tenants and sub-tenants belong to this category."

The aforesaid issues are not taken into account while compensating the displaced persons. Moreover, compensation for land acquisition is indicated as an element of total project cost. But in fact, displacement involves several other type of sasts risk like (i) Landlessness (ii) Joblessness (iii) Homelessness (iv) Marginalisation (v) Increased morbidity (vi) Food insecurity (vii) Less of access to common property etc.

Multiple Displacement

Because of displacement, the oustees undergo an acute psychological, physical economic trauma as well as an identity crisis. The oustees face untold problems due to multiple displacement. The inhuman tragedy and plight of oustees of Hindustan Aeronautics Limited (HAL), Hirakud Dam Project, can be well conceived as illustrations of this Multiple displacement. The HAL oustees displaced during 1960s for the first time, constrained for displacement in 1980s second time due to Upper Kolab Multi-purpose Dam Project. The

Rihand Dam oustees were displaced first by the dam itself, then by coal mines, then again by thermal plants and finally when the government declared their colony was forest land. Similarly, the oustees of Hirakud Dam Project who were displaced in the mid-1950s and resettled in Brajarajnagar area of Jharsuguda district, confronted displacement for the second time because of construction of the Ib Thermal Power Station in the late 1980s.

Though the development of economy and the region is intended by such dam projects and other developmental projects, but acute problems have been caused especially tribals, small farmers and marginal farmers.

It is inferred from the analysis that the development projects and river dam projects restricted the community right over natural resources, rich forest areas have been exploited and tribal inhabitants and original habitants of the project area have been vulnerable to exploitation and pauperization.

In this context it is imperative that the NGO should play an active role in mobilizing people and tribals to protect the resources, habitant and the tribals, and must actively cooperate in their resettlement programmes. The rehabilitation programme should be genuine, just and must minimise the suffering of the people.

REFERENCES

1. Fernades, W. (1994): *Development induced Displacement in the Tribal Areas of Eastern India*, New Delhi, Indian Social Institute (Mimeo).
2. Pachauri, R.K. (2000), Might of Contention (A Damed Model of Development) *The Times of India*, 17th November.
3. Pandey, Balaji (2000), Protection of right to livelihood and survival of the development induced displaced persons in Orissa: A note for discussion, *Vision* (Vol. XIX. Nos. 3-4) pp. 94-95.
4. Kar, G.C. (1999), Displacement, Resettlement and Rehabilitation, *Orissa Economic Journal*, Vol . XXXI, No. 1 & 2, p. 19.

Index

A

Africa, 35

Akhil Bhartiya Adivasi Vikas Parishad, 26, 30

Amar Singh, 62

Amte, Baba, 65

Andhra Pradesh, 8, 12, 129, 133, 134

Anjanwala, 55

Arjun Singh, 65

Arunachal Pradesh, 176

Arunachal University, 176

Asaf Ali, Mr., 162

B

Balimela Dam Project, 10

Balimela HydroElectric Project, 14, 16

Bargarh, 36, 155

Bargi Dam Project, 36

Bay of Bengal, 2, 133

Beas, 93

Behera, Surendra Nath, 179

Bellamy John, 17

Bhakra, 1

Bhadrachalam, 13

Bhakras, 93

Bhilai Steel Plant, 129

Bhutan, 7

Bonda Development Agency, 14

Brahmani, 2

Bruntland Commission, 95

Budhafalnga, 2

C

Calcutta, 116

Central Cattle Breeding Farm, 23

Central Sector Projects, 7

Central Water Irrigation and Navigation Commission, 162

Central Water and Power Commission, 15, 16, 55, 60

Chhatisgarh, 133, 134

Chhatisgarh Government, 36

Chukk H.E. Project, 7

Clugh, Dr., 62

Commission of Environment and Development Report, 75

Common Property Resources, 107, 113, 125, 170

Congress (I), 64

D

Dalua, 8, 29

Damanjodi, 105, 106

Damodar Valley, 1
Dams and Minor Irrigation Projects, 181
Dandakaranya Development . Authority, 27, 185
Das, C.R., 99
Dasarda, H.M., 69
Dehradun, 93
Delhi, 67, 88
Dongria Kondh Development Agency, 13
Draft National Policy of Rehabilitation, 172
Duduma River, 8

E

Earthquake Engineering School, 62
Eighth Five Year Plan, 63
Environmental Defence Fund, 65
Environmental Policy Institute, 65

F

Faster, 175
Fernades, Mr., 130, 131, 138
Fernades, Walter, 182
First Famine Commission, 53

G

Gajapati District, 37
Gandhi, Indira, 94, 105, 106, 122
Gandhi, Rajiv, 63, 74
Godavari, 12
Godoghati, 12
Gujarat, 52-55, 58, 60-63, 74, 88, 91, 92, 96, 129, 190

H

Harvey, 175
Himalayas, 93
Hindustan Aeronautics Ltd., 192
Hirakud, 16, 155, 158, 160, 164
Hirakud Dam Project, 9, 36, 121, 139, 151, 152, 158, 159, 192, 193
Hirakud Dam Project Report, 152, 162
Hirakud Hydro-Power Dam Project, 129
Hirakud Land Organisation, 164
Hydro-Electric Multi-Purpose Project, 137, 146
Hydro Power Projects, 6

I

Ib Thermal Power Station, 193
Impoverishment, Risk and Reconstruction, 169, 170, 172
India, 1, 3, 32, 39, 43, 44, 52, 57, 86, 87, 94, 116, 129, 138, 182, 188, 189
India Country Study, 69
Indian Agricultural Economy Conference, 69
Indian Institute of Public Administration, 187
Indian Social Institute, 187
Indravati river, 11
Institute of Social Sciences, 75
International Commission on Large Dams, 145

J

J.K. Paper Mill, 14
Jaipur, 16, 20

Japan, 65
Jawahar Water Works Sunabeda, 23
Jharsuguda District, 193
Jojo, Bipin Kumar Dr., 1

K

Kalahandi, 11, 180
Katadia, Manuthai, 62
Keonjhar, 10, 134
Khargone District, 54
Kolab river, 12
Koraput, 11-14, 17, 22, 23, 26, 27, 97, 137, 180
Koronga, 12
Kosi, 1
Kothari, Rajni, 59

L

Land Acquisition Act, 25, 101-103, 115, 116, 119, 120, 122, 124, 125
Land Aquisition Review Committee, 101
Law Commission, 101
Local Displaced Persons, 108

M

Machkund Hydro-Project, 8, 9, 14, 16, 137
Madhya Pradesh, 12, 53-55, 66, 67, 74, 75, 92, 96, 129, 190
Mahanadi, 1, 2, 36
Mahapatra Mr., 9, 130-132
Maharaja of Jeypore, 8
Maharastra, 53-55, 64, 65, 67, 75, 88, 96
Medha Patkar, 64
Michael Carnea, 169
Mining Project, 148
Minister's Special Assistance Programme, 14
Mishra, Deepak K. Dr., 166
Mohanty, Ranjita Kumari, Smt., 179

N

Nalco, 14, 104-113, 122
NGOs, 12, 145, 193
Nagaland, 133
Narmada, 36, 52, 53, 89, 93
Narmada Bachao Andolan, 11, 61, 64, 66, 67, 189, 190
Narmada Control Authority, 75
Narmada Dam Project, 190
Narmada Multi-purpose Project, 85
Narmada Power Project, 91
Narmada Sagar Project, 61, 64, 89, 93
Narmada Valley, 52, 67, 69, 73
Narmada Valley Development Authority, 67, 73, 74
Narmada Valley Project, 40, 52-56, 58, 59, 64, 74, 76, 89, 93, 188, 189
Narmada Water Disputes Tribunal, 53, 55, 61, 63, 68, 73
Nath, G.D., 115
National Commission on SC & ST, 180
National Geo-physical Research Institute, 67
National Policy for Rehabilitation, 44

Upper Indiravati Project, 12
Upper Kolab Multi-purpose Project, 2, 11, 12, 14-18, 20-23, 25-27, 29-32, 137, 180, 192
Uttar Pradesh, 88

V

Varma, S.S., Mr., 75

W

Washington, 69
West Bengal, 133, 134
Wordsworth William, 52
World Bank, 10, 11, 62, 63, 65-68, 115, 130, 144, 145, 169
World Commission on Dams, 39, 69, 75, 86, 144, 145, 188

❑❑❑

National Wild Life Federation, 65
Negi, Prasant, 52
Nehru Jawahar Lal 53, 57, 121, 129, 152
New Delhi, 187
Non-Timber Forest Produce, 181
Nowrangpur, 13

O

Official Secret Act, 62
Orissa, 2, 3, 6, 7-9, 11-14, 18, 39, 100, 104, 105, 115, 122, 128, 129, 131, 133-139, 144, 146, 148, 151-153, 156, 157, 162, 190
Orissa Power System, 16
Orissa Small Industries Corporation, 23

P

Patel, Sardar, 60
Planning Commission, 60, 69, 88, 93
Planning Commission Report, 59
Postel Sandra, Mr., 69
Pottern Irrigation Dam Project, 37
Prime Minister's Rojgar Yojna, 97
Primitive Tribal Group, 134
Project Affected People, 106, 108, 109, 171

R

Railway Act, 103
Railways, 8
Rajasthan, 88
Ramganga, 93
Ramkrishna, A., 42
Rayagada, 15
Rehabilitation Advisory Committee, 22, 26, 27
Resettlement and Rehabilitation Programme, 22
River Dam Project, 187
Rourkela, 16, 123
Rural Organizations, 64

S

Saintala Ordnance Industry, 124
Salandi, 2
Salandi Irrigation Project, 10
Sambalpur, 9
Sarabhai, Mrinalini, Mrs., 74
Sardar Sarovar Narmada Nigam, 61, 62
Sardar Sarovar Project, 53, 85, 88-93, 96, 144
Satpathi, Nandini, Smt., 18
Satiguda Dam, 20
Seventh Five Year Plan, 20
Special Land Acquisition Act, 157
Stanely, Mr., 9
Subaranpur, 36
Subarnarekha, 2
Substained Affected Persons, 108
Summani Nimat Khan, 307
Supreme Court, 66, 101
Swaminathan, Dr., 63

T

Talcher Thermal Station, 16, 17
Tehri Dam Project, 37, 85, 90
Tripathy, S.N., 35
Tripathy, Sadasiv, 154

U

United States, 65